The Birthday Party BOOK

From Your First to Your 100th Birthday

Diane Ross and Elyse Schaffer

HAMMOND INCORPORATED   MAPLEWOOD, NEW JERSEY

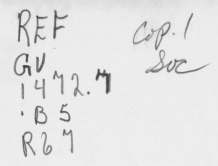
DEDICATION

Dedicated to April 19th, May 27th, July 12th,
August 23rd, August 31st and November 27th.

Library of Congress Cataloging in Publication Data
Ross, Diane.
  Birthday party book.

   1. Entertaining. 2. Birthdays. I. Schaffer,
Elyse, joint author. II. Title.
GV1472.7.B5R67 793.2 78-5390
ISBN 0-8437-2801-9

Printed in the United States of America

CONTENTS

INTRODUCTION

You Are Never Too Old or Too Young
to Have a Birthday Party

This is your life. Why not enjoy giving or having a birthday party. Not only are they fun to have or give, but they are fun to attend. Birthday parties are not only for the little ones, they are for big people as well. As a matter of fact, the best birthday parties come in later years when people truly appreciate their lives. Of course, a birthday party for a young child would be entirely different than a birthday party for an adult, but either type is loads of fun if planned properly.

When was the last time you, as an adult, had a special birthday party — something to remember for years to come? We all enjoy being fussed over or making a fuss for someone near and dear to us. And what about that priceless look on somebody's face when one walks in the door and everyone yells "Surprise"?

Opportunity knocks but once a year, so why not take advantage of this fact and give a birthday party. It shows someone you care, the rewards are countless and, besides, you can become the talk of the town. Furthermore, it really doesn't take much effort — just a little planning and creativity.

This book will guide you in planning simple and successful parties. It gives many novel ideas for unusual parties for people ages 1-100. These ideas, whether they be given for the children's or adult's birthday parties, can be modified to fit anyone. Each section will tell you all the things you need to know when planning a party and gives easy-to-follow instructions for everything from invitations to the cake.

CHAPTER I

The Basics

The amount of time, energy and care put into a party will greatly affect its results. Careful planning will do much to make your party a success. Additionally, the success of a party depends on the attitude of the host and/or hostess. Be relaxed and be yourself and it will reflect upon your guests, thus making them feel as relaxed as you. A party may be as simple or elaborate as you choose. A party is not made to impress people, but to entertain them; so have fun along with your guests. Getting down to the basics is the first and most important item on the agenda.

Theme

When planning a party, the first decision to be made is the theme you will use. There are an infinite number of ideas that can be used and there are several ways to go about choosing one. Think about the people you intend to invite to your party — do they have any common interests that can be used as a theme? If the party is for a child, ask the child what type of party he or she would like to have, or use one of his primary interests as a theme. Additionally, looking through magazines or books and watching television can give you ideas. A party theme can be designed around almost anything, whether it be a tree or a particular sport; the whole party, from beginning to end, should reflect this theme.

After deciding on a theme, think about how to relate everything needed for the party to the theme you have chosen.

Guest List

A guest list should be prepared so you will know how many invitations are needed. When making the list, consider how many people you can handle. Remember, two is company, three is a crowd. Do you want a small, more intimate party or a large, gala affair? Also, consider the size of the room to be used for the party — you don't want it to be overcrowded.

Invitations

After planning the guest list, design or purchase invitations to go along with the theme. If you prepare invitations, they don't have to be elaborate and you don't have to be Michelangelo. However, don't forget to include the following information: name, day and date, time (if for a meal, say so), address and RSVP (give response date and telephone number). If it is a surprise party, this should be mentioned on the invitation. There is nothing more disappointing than planning a surprise party and finding that the guest of honor knows about it.

Mail the invitations for a children's party two weeks before the party and for an adult's party three to four weeks before. This gives the guests some time to make arrangements to attend. If the party is planned around a holiday, more notice might be needed. The RSVP date should be one week before the party so that you have enough time to prepare.

Decorations

Don't get in over your head with room decorations. By keeping them simple, everyone can help with the decorating. Children, especially, enjoy helping.

A space should be provided for activities whether it be in the room with the decorated table or in another room. If possible, have a small table off in a corner of the room for the gifts, since often when people attend a party nobody knows where to put them. If you are serving a meal, prepare a seating arrangement prior to the party so there will be no confusion when it is time for everyone to sit down at the table.

Food

The food prepared for the party does not have to be an elaborate feast; do as much or as little as you enjoy doing. Relate the food to the theme of the party by thinking of zany names for each dish or designing and decorating it appropriately. Birthday parties do not have to include a meal. Particularly for a children's party, cake, maybe some ice cream and a drink are sufficient. The cake cannot be done without and it should be something special.

Games and Party Favors

Second only to cake, games or a special activity are an important ingredient of a children's party. Prizes for the winners are not necessary. Their "prize" can be going first in the next game. Even adults enjoy playing games since we are all young at heart to some extent. In addition, games break the ice when you have a variety of people at a party, whether they be children or adults.

Favors are not necessary at a children's party but they certainly are well appreciated. The favors can be given to the children as they leave, serving as a memento of the party.

Schedules

Having planned the games and favors, you will be able to organize a party schedule which will keep the party running smoothly. Here is an example of a children's birthday party schedule:

1. Play a participation game with the children until all the guests have arrived. (15 minutes)
2. Serve the food, if the party calls for it. (30 minutes)
3. Tell a story to calm the children down. (15 minutes)
4. Have a special activity such as a clown or magician. (45 minutes)
5. Serve the cake (and ice cream). (30 minutes)
6. Play another game. (15 minutes)
7. Open the gifts (as long as all guests have brought one). (30 minutes)
8. Have on hand one or two extra games in case there is time left.

"The best laid schemes o' mice and men . . ." can often go astray so be prepared to vary your schedule a little if necessary. Also, when it's time for K.P., let the children do their share (they love to help). Ask for volunteers to throw away paper goods after they are used. Do this during the party and after the presents are opened before proceeding to the next activity so that there is less work for you later. You'll be surprised at how many helpers you will have. This is a good way to involve shy children in the activities.

A schedule for any party helps to keep the party running smoothly, therefore, an adult birthday party warrants a schedule as well as the abovementioned schedule for a children's party. The following is a general schedule for an adult's party:
1. Cocktail hour (1 hour — 1½ hours)
2. Special activity (1½ hours — 2 hours)
3. Dessert (½ hour)
4. Open the gifts (as long as all guests have brought one) (½ hour)

Thank You Notes

When party day has passed, it is a proper gesture to send thank you notes for all the gifts. Even children can write their own thank you notes if they are old enough.

For very young people, an alternative is to prepare thank you notes before the party saying "Thank you for coming to my party. I hope you had a good time." These can be given out with the favors.

CHAPTER II

Birthday Parties for the Nursery Set (Ages 1-5)

When planning a birthday party for a one- or two-year-old, you must keep in mind that children of this age cannot be expected to play organized games or even to eat all the foods served at the party. However, there are usually some older children present who will need to be entertained with games and other activities. A wee tot of one or two will need his mother to remain at the party to tend to the feeding and caring for him.

As for three- to five-year-olds, through our experiences, we have found that a birthday party for these children works best when the mothers of the children are not present. Many times they relax and listen better to someone other than their own mothers. We know that it is not always possible to hold a birthday party without other moms present, but the party will probably run smoother if they are not there.

A good idea, however, is to have a babysitter or a friend to help out at the party. The mothers can be invited back for coffee and cake when they come to pick up their children. When planning a party for young children, keep in mind that, like their height, their attention span is usually short; therefore, you will probably have to change activities every fifteen minutes.

Purchase paper goods — tablecloth, napkins, plates and cups — to go along with the colors or theme of your party. Choose a book or other item relating to the theme that can be used as a centerpiece for the table. All the decorating can be done the day before the party, thus making everything a lot easier for you on the day itself. For all of the following themes, we have provided information on making invitations, decorations and favors, types of food to serve, designing the birthday cake and preparing games and other special activities.

THE CIRCUS COMES TO TOWN

"Ladies and gentlemen, children of all ages . . ." All people, especially children, look forward to the circus coming to town. The circus is an all-time favorite party theme, and Mom's magic can turn the house into a big top to the wonderment of all.

Invitations

Who is the most popular performer in the circus? The clown; and what is a circus without one? You can use part of the clown costume for the invitations and the wording can be like a circus flyer. Invitations should be simple so the birthday child or any brothers or sisters can help make them. For each invitation:

1. Use colorful oak tag paper and cut out a triangle 3½" x 6¼" x 6¼" (see fig. 1).

fig. 1

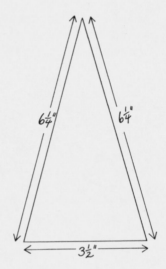

2. Paste a small cotton ball or a fringe ball (small pom pom) to the top of the triangle.
3. Along the bottom of the triangle, apply a strip of glue. Sprinkle glitter over the glue. If glitter is unavailable, you can use sequins, birdseed or spices for the bottom of the hat.
4. The following is a sample wording for the completed clown hat invitation.

THE CIRCUS IS COMING TO TOWN
HOPE YOU CAN JOIN IN!!
LIMITED ENGAGEMENT: Saturday, Dec. 1st
12:30-3:30 (Lunch)
BIG TOP: 1 Main Street, Anywhere, U.S.A.
RINGMASTER: Jane Doe
RSVP: (1 week before party)
(telephone number)
When completed, this hat will fit into a No. 6¾ size envelope
(3⅝" x 6½").

Decorations

To get into the circus mood, decorate the room to look like a big top. Use four old flat sheets (twin-size will do) if available; paint broad red stripes down their length. Gather the width of each sheet at one end and tack the gathered ends to the center of the ceiling with the stripes facing the floor. Take the remaining two corners of each sheet and tack them either to two corners of the ceiling or just over the table(s). Be sure the sheets are draped somewhat. If sheets are not available, you can use crepe paper streamers to get the same effect. Take groups of three long streamers and gather them together at one end and tape to the center of the ceiling. Spread the three other ends equally to cover one-quarter of the ceiling. Do this three more times so the whole area is covered. Inflate brightly colored balloons to provide one for each little person attending the party. Attach a string to each balloon. Gather the strings together and hang them in the center of the big top.

Most circuses have a sideshow (place where the animals are kept before the show). You can easily have one, too. In one corner of the room, set up a small table and place on it a number of stuffed animals such as bears, lions, elephants, monkeys, dogs and horses. Hang streamers straight down from the ceiling to the floor in front of the table so that they give the appearance of a cage. Make a sign for the sideshow area saying, "No Feeding, Please."

For information on the table decor, see the introduction to this chapter.

Favors

A Clown Holder/Bank is a very simple, useful and attractive item which will serve to remind your guests of the circus party. It has a hat upon which you can write a child's name and thus can be used to indicate the seating arrangements, thereby eliminating pushing or shoving for seats and it will also serve as a table decoration. You can put candy, prizes or a few crayons in it as part of the favor.

Clown Holder/Bank

1 small can with lid for each clown
   (i.e., ready-made frosting can or peanut can)
   white self-adhesive vinyl or other washable material
   felt scraps for features on clown face
1 fringe ball
1 birthday hat
   felt-tip marking pen
   glue
   scissors
Remove paper from the can. Wash and dry the can thoroughly. Cut the self-adhesive material 1" higher than the height of the can and wide enough to go around it. Cover the can with the self-adhesive material and

tuck the excess into the top of the can. If necessary, trim the bottom. Cut out the clown features from felt scraps as illustrated in fig. 2. Glue features onto can with eartabs glued to either side of the can. Cut a slot in the center of the plastic lid so the can may be used as a bank. Place lid on the can. Write a child's name on the birthday hat with a felt-tip marking pen. Place hat on top of the can with the elastic going around the bottom.

fig. 2

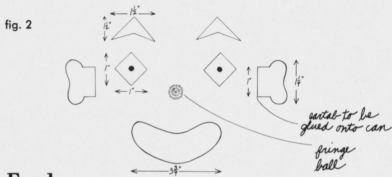

eartab to be glued onto can

fringe ball

Food

Clownwiches

2 slices white bread per sandwich
  peanut butter
  jelly

1 large marshmallow
raisins

Cut the bread into triangles (see fig. 3). Spread one triangle with a layer of peanut butter and then a layer of jelly. Place the other bread triangle on top of the first. Use peanut butter to stick marshmallow to the top point of the triangle and to stick raisins on the bread as decorations.

fig. 3

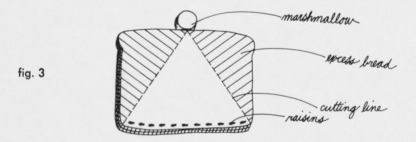

marshmallow

excess bread

cutting line
raisins

Giraffe Carafe

Slice off the top of a marshmallow diagonally to make a giraffe head. Use the excess piece of marshmallow to make two ears by cutting it in half and sticking one piece to each side of the marshmallow. Push the end of a straw into the bottom and put the straw in a glass of milk.

Funny Hat Cake

1 package cake mix, any flavor
1 can prepared frosting in a light color
  chocolate chips or colored gumdrops

colored sprinkles
coconut (optional)
food coloring (optional)

Prepare cake according to package directions, using a 13" x 9" pan. Let cake cool. Remove from pan and cut out cake according to illustration in fig. 4. Cover a cookie sheet with aluminum foil and place cut pieces of cake on cookie sheet as illustrated in fig. 5. Use frosting to hold pieces together. Frost cake and decorate as shown in fig. 5. If desired, sprinkle tinted coconut on the cookie sheet surounding the cake. (To color coconut, place coconut in a plastic bag, put a few drops of food coloring in any color you wish in the bag with the coconut and shake the bag well.) Sprinkle the coconut on individual pieces of cake for those children who like it.

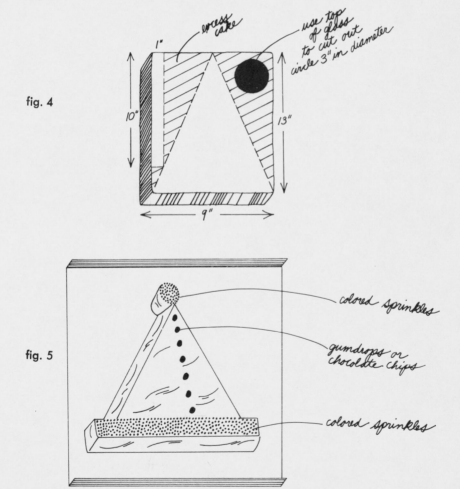

fig. 4

fig. 5

Games

Pin the Pom Pom on the Clown

Draw a clown face with a cone-shaped hat on a large piece of heavy paper. Hang the picture on a wall. Give each child a cotton ball with a piece of masking tape attached to it. Make sure a piece of the tape extends from the cotton ball so the children can stick it to the picture. Masking tape is recommended because other tapes tend to pull paint off the wall in case there's a miss.

One at a time, blindfold each child and face him or her in the direction of the picture. Have the child walk toward the picture and stick the cotton ball as close to the top of the hat as he or she can. The child who comes the closest to the top of the hat is the winner.

Throw the Ball (or Beanbag) Through the Nose

Draw a clown face on a large piece of cardboard or oak tag. Cut out a hole where the nose is supposed to be. Make it rather large so that the children will be able to throw a small ball through it without too much difficulty. Hang the cardboard or oak tag clown face from the ceiling with a string. Be sure it is low enough so the children can reach it when they throw a foam rubber ball or a bean bag.

Special Activity

As a special treat, you can hire a clown or a magician for entertainment. The amateurs in this field are usually very reasonable, and they keep the children busy. If you do not wish to hire a clown, have someone dress up as one. There are many types of clowns; one of the easiest to create is a hobo clown. He wears old clothes with patches and an old hat. He can either wear makeup or just have dirty smudges rubbed on his face. If someone dresses up as a clown for the party, here are a few suggestions:

1. The clown can carry a bag of plastic charms, lollipops, balloons or any other small trinkets, and the children can put their hands into the bag and reach for a surprise.
2. The clown can also be a storyteller and read the circus book being used as the table centerpiece.

FUN AT THE ZOO

Today's children are surrounded with animations, puppets and toys in the form of animals. Many of their favorites from books, TV or the movies are fuzzy creatures, or yaks, anteaters, aardvarks, et al. from the animal world. Faster than Noah, a zoo party can gather together the animal kingdom to fascinate and entertain the guests.

Invitations

Bingo, the Birthday Bear can announce to all that a special day at the zoo is coming. You're not artistic? Find pictures in children's coloring books or storybooks to use as a pattern. So as not to ruin a book, take a piece of white tracing paper and trace the animal's face.

1. For each bear invitation, use brown construction paper. Fold the paper in half widthwise and then cut down the middle to make two folded papers 4½" x 6", with the fold on the 4½" edge and on top (see fig. 1).

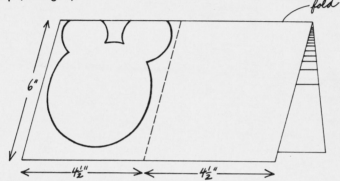

fig. 1

2. Cut out the traced picture of the animal face.
3. Place on folded construction paper with the ears touching the fold line.
4. Draw the outline of the face.
5. Cut out the face through the two layers of paper, being sure *not* to cut the top of the ears where the fold connects the front to the back.
6. Use buttons for the eyes and nose and use string or yarn for the mouth (see fig. 2).

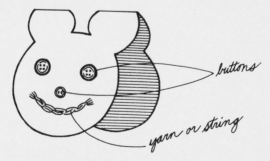

fig. 2

7. Wording for the invitation can be written on the inside part of the face.

BINGO, THE BIRTHDAY BEAR, INVITES YOU TO
VISIT THE ZOO ON: (day and date)
FEEDING TIME: (time of party and if for a meal)
CAGE: (address)
HEAD ZOOKEEPER: (name)
RSVP: (date and telephone number)

Decorations

The easiest and most inexpensive way to decorate the room is by making posters and signs. Construction paper can be used here, too. Suggested signs: Welcome to the (last name) Zoo (place this near the entrance door), Monkey Cage This Way (with an arrow pointing into the party room), Please Do Not Feed the Animals, Balloon Man and Keep Hands Off. Next to a mirror, put a sign that says, Extinct Animal. Have the children look at themselves in the mirror and explain the meaning of an extinct animal.

Find big pictures of animals and hang them on the wall. Hang streamers straight down from the ceiling to the floor in front of the animal pictures to give the effect of a cage. Hang a "Please Do Not Feed the Animals" sign under or next to the cage. If you have any stuffed animals in the house, they can be used to decorate the room by sitting them on tables or shelves.

Balloons are always festive, and there are many things that can be done with them. One suggestion is to purchase plain balloons or those in the shapes of animal heads and attach them to thin dowels. Make sure there are enough balloons for everyone. Group the balloons and place them in a corner of the room or on a wall.

A deep box can be decorated as a cage for the table centerpiece and used as a storage place for the favors.

Favors

Since the party room is going to be a zoo, zookeeper hats for the guests will be appropriate and are very simple to make.

1. Use 9" x 12" construction paper. For each hat, cut one sheet in half the long way and trim to 4" height (see fig. 3).

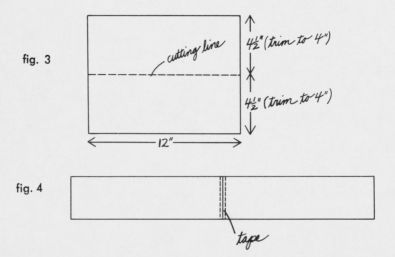

fig. 3

cutting line

4½" (trim to 4")

4½" (trim to 4")

12"

fig. 4

tape

2. Lay the two strips end-to-end and tape together on both the inside and outside (see fig. 4).
3. Bring the two free ends around and tape together to form a circle. Use the head of the birthday child as a guide for the size. Write "Zookeeper" on the front of the hats for the guests and "Head Zookeeper" on the birthday child's hat.
4. Trace a circle 6½" in diameter onto construction paper and cut out. Cut the circle in half and use one-half as a visor for the hat.
5. Make a fold along the straight edge of the half-circle 1" from the edge (see fig. 5).

fig. 5

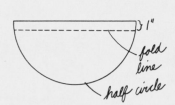

fig. 6

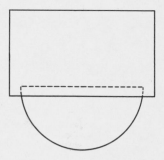

6. Tape the half-circle to the inside of the hat up to the fold line, as shown in fig. 6, leaving the remainder of the half-circle extending outward to form the visor of the hat.

A favor that the children can take home is the Caged Animal Beanbag. Every time the children play with their beanbags, they will have happy memories of your party.

Caged Animal Beanbag

scraps of fabric (two pieces, 4¾" x 6", for each beanbag)
bias tape (½" wide)
felt scraps
birdseed (for filling)
needle and thread
straight pins
scissors

Draw animal on felt, using pattern in fig. 7 as a guide. Cut out the animal and paste onto right side of one piece of fabric with the long side as the width (see fig. 8). Cut bias tape into three pieces 4¾" in length and pin in place over the animal, spacing equally to give the effect of a cage. Be sure the ends of the tape are pinned to the edges of the fabric.

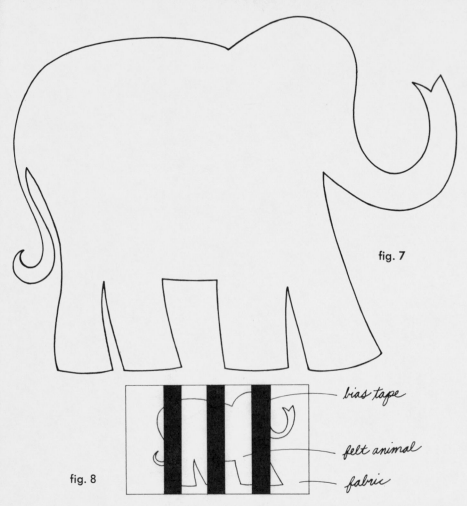

fig. 7

fig. 8

bias tape

felt animal

fabric

Pin the two pieces of fabric right sides together. Sew around three sides, leaving a ⅝" seam allowance and being sure to catch the bias tape in the seam. Turn right-side-out and fill one-half to three-quarters full with birdseed. Tuck in seam allowance on open end and sew together on outside. If sewing by hand, be sure your stiches are small so the birdseed wil not fall out.

Food

Zookeepers' Lunch

Serve hot dogs in buns, peanuts and/or popcorn. A novel twist is to put the peanuts or popcorn into a bucket with the words "Animal Food" written on it. Serve each child from the bucket.

Zebra Soda

Fill each glass half-full with chocolate or cola soft drink. Add one scoop of vanilla ice cream. Stir gently and serve.

Piggly Wiggly Cake

1 package cake mix, any flavor
2 chocolate-covered mints
2 raisins
1 can prepared frosting (strawberry, cherry or vanilla
    tinted pink)

1 Drake's Ring Ding cake
1 piece red string licorice
4 pipe cleaners

Prepare cake according to package directions, using two 8" or 9" round
cake pans. Let cakes cool. Frost one layer of cake on top and sides;
place second layer on top of first and frost entire cake, saving ½ cup of
frosting. Place Ring Ding on top of cake in the center for nose. Cover the
Ring Ding with frosting. Use the two raisins for nostrils. Above frosted Ring
Ding, place the two chocolate-covered mints for eyes (see fig. 9). Use
licorice to form mouth. Form pipe cleaners into pig-shaped ears and put
ends into cake as shown in fig. 9, pushing them in near the top edge of
the cake.

fig. 9

Games

How Many Peanuts in the Bucket?

Put peanuts in a bucket and have the children guess how many there
are. The one who comes the closest is the winner.

Duck, Duck, Goose

This game is an old favorite for young children. Have the children
sit in a circle with one child standing outside the circle as the "goose."
The "goose" walks around the circle and touches each child's head and
says "duck" or "goose" as he touches each head. If he says "duck" he
keeps going; when he touches a head and says "goose," that child gets
up and runs after the "goose" while the "goose" runs around the outside
of the circle to the child's place in the circle. If the "goose" is tagged before he reaches the place in the circle, he remains the "goose." If he is
not tagged, the other child becomes the new "goose." Play continues in
this fashion for as long as you desire.

Put the Elephant in His Cage

On a piece of oak tag paper 14" x 22" draw bars from top of the paper to bottom. Draw a door on the cage 5" wide and 8" high. Cut elephants out of construction paper, using the pattern given for the Caged Animal Beanbag favors. Hang the cage on the wall and give each child an elephant with a piece of masking tape extending from the top. Blindfold one child at a time and face him or her in the direction of the cage. Let the child walk to the cage and try to stick the elephant on the door of the cage. The one who sticks an elephant closest to the door is the winner.

Special Activity

Visit to the Zoo

Going to the zoo always makes a big impression on children. If you live near a zoo, your little guests would enjoy visiting it. If you decide to go to the zoo, just serve the cake and go. The games and even lunch can be eliminated.

Draw the Funniest Animal

Give each child a piece of cardboard or heavy paper and crayons. Ask the children to draw the funniest animal they can. If any of them have trouble, join in the fun and help draw the pictures. After they have all finished, write each child's name on his or her picture and cut the cardboard at random into four pieces. Each child will have a personalized puzzle, which can be put into a small plastic bag and taken home.

SHAPE—O'S

Those most receptive and eager to learn are the little children. There's so much to absorb in the world around them, and every day in their lives new doors to knowledge are opening. A birthday party that teaches and involves is often more fun and successful than others. Through the use of colors and shapes, concepts easy for all to grasp, this party can be a real winner.

Invitations

A traffic light combines a rectangle and circles and the colors red, yellow and green. It can also be used to teach the little ones about street-crossing safety. For each invitation:

1. Using 9" x 12" white construction paper, fold sheets in half lengthwise. Cut 1" off the long edge of the paper as shown. Cut the folded paper in half to form two folded rectangles 3½" x 6" as in fig. 1.
2. Hold the paper with the fold on left and make three circles (about 1¾" diameter) down the front, one under the other. After

writing the following on the outside, color the circles to look like traffic lights (one red, one yellow and one green).

fig. 1

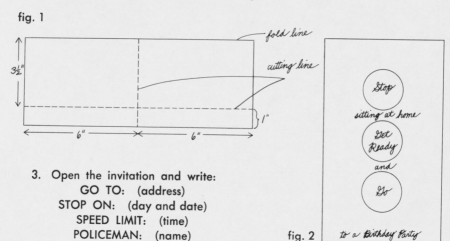

3. Open the invitation and write:
    GO TO: (address)
    STOP ON: (day and date)
    SPEED LIMIT: (time)
    POLICEMAN: (name)

fig. 2

Decorations

From colored construction paper, cut out shapes (circle, rectangle, triangle, etc.) and write down the color and name of the shape on it. Hang these shapes all over the room. Blow up enough balloons in different colors and shapes for everyone and hang them all over the room.

Use a white tablecloth and tape a variety of colored shapes on it down the center of the table. Make a mobile from wire hangers, string with colored shapes and hang it over the table for a centerpiece.

Create name tags for the guests, using small colored shapes and safety pins to pin them on. Of course, many of the children may not be able to read the names, but they can name the shapes and colors.

Favors

Since a traffic light is used as the invitation, you can follow through by making policeman's caps for party hats.
1. Using 9" x 12" dark blue construction paper, cut one sheet for each cap in half lengthwise and trim both strips to a 4" height (see fig. 3).

fig. 3

2. Lay the two strips end-to-end and tape together inside and out (see fig. 4).

fig. 4

tape

3. Bring the two free ends around and tape together to form a circle. Use the head of the birthday child as a guide for the size. Write each child's name on the front of the hat with a light crayon.
4. Trace a circle 6½" in diameter onto dark blue construction paper and cut out. Cut the circle in half and use one-half as a visor for the hat.
5. Make a fold along the straight edge of the half-circle 1" from the edge (see fig. 5).

fig. 5   fig. 6

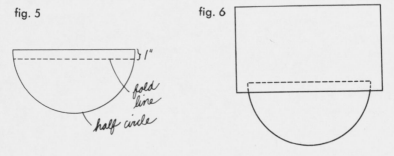

6. Tape the half-circle to the inside of the hat up to the fold line, as shown in fig. 6, leaving the remainder of the half-circle extending outward to form the visor of the hat.

   Children enjoy looking at books. You can give them a fun book to take home from the party.

Shape-O Book

1 piece oak tag cut into 6" x 9" pieces
    (a 22" x 28" piece of oak tag will make 9 6" x 9" pieces)
2 pieces of ribbon (about 8" each)
  scraps of solid-color fabric of varied textures
  colored construction paper
  glue
  scissors

For each book, take four pieces of oak tag and punch two holes on the left side of each piece for binding the book. Slip ribbon through the holes and tie each one, leaving some space for turning the pages. For each cover, cut out six different shapes about 1" high and wide. Write one letter in each shape to spell out the word "SHAPE-O". Paste this on the cover diagonally, writing in the hyphen. Turn the cover page and leave the left side blank. On the right side, glue one of the shapes. Write the name and color of the shape under it. Number the pages to help the children learn their numbers. Continue doing this on the next four pages. Here are some types of shapes that can be used: circle, square, rectangle, triangle, octagon, trapezoid, rhombus, oval, semicircle.

Food

Shapee Sandwich

Make sandwiches with any filling you desire. Cut the sandwiches into different shapes such as the following:

diamond   semicircle   square   rectangle   triangle

Give each child at least two different shapes. Before they eat their sandwiches, you can play a little game with shapes. Ask them "Who has a rectangle?" (square, etc.). The one with the shape named raises his hand.

Cylinder Drink

Serve chocolate milk in cylindrical glasses.

Stop, Look and Listen Cake

1 package cake mix, any flavor
2 cans ready-made frosting (1 dark chocolate & 1 vanilla)
   food coloring (red, yellow, green)
3 Hostess Big Wheel cakes
Prepare cake mix according to package directions, using a 13" x 9" pan. Let cake cool. Frost entire cake with chocolate frosting. Gently press the Hostess Big Wheel cakes into the top of the cake, one under the other down the center, spacing them evenly to look like a traffic light. Take ¼ cup white frosting for each of the 3 Big Wheels. Tint ¼ cup red, ¼ cup yellow and ¼ cup green. Frost the top of the first Big Wheel with red frosting; frost the top of the second Big Wheel with yellow and frost the third with green.

Games

Red Light, Green Light

This is an old favorite for young children. Have the children form a line, with one child being "It" and facing the line at the opposite end of the room. "It" turns his back and says "Red light, green light, one, two, three" and then turns around. When the child's back is turned and he or she is counting, everyone tries to tap "It" by moving as close as possible. When "It" says "Red light, green light, one, two, three" he or she turns around and, if "It" catches anybody moving, that person goes back to the start. "It" then turns his back again and counts. If someone taps "It" when "Its" back is turned, everyone runs back to start, with "It" trying to tap someone before they all get there. Whoever is tapped becomes "It." If no one is tapped, the same person is "It" again.

Pin the Red Light on the Traffic Signals

On a large rectangular piece of black cardboard or oak tag, glue three circles — one red, one yellow and one green — to give the appearance of a traffic light. Cut out enough red circles for everyone and write each child's name on a circle. Attach a strip of masking tape to each circle, leaving a piece of tape extending from it. Blindfold each child one at a time, and face him or her in the direction of the traffic light. The one who sticks the red light the closest to its spot is the winner.

Touch and Tell

Collect a number of objects in different shapes (a ball, a square box, a ball of yarn, a block of any shape, cardboard in any shape, fruit). Put one item in a paper bag. Have a child put his hand in the bag without looking and try to guess the shape of the object. Continue doing this with each child, changing the object for each.

Special Activity

Children have a lot of respect for policemen and visiting the police station will leave a great impression on them. Call up your local police station and ask if you may bring the children to visit the police station. As you are going to the police station, point out the different shaped signs.

HUMPTY DUMPTY

Do you remember some of those nursery rhymes you loved as a child? Humpty Dumpty is a favorite. For those who have forgotten the Humpty Dumpty nursery rhyme, it goes as follows:

Humpty Dumpty sat on a wall,
Humpty Dumpty had a great fall.
All the King's horses and all the King's men,
Couldn't put Humpty together again.

Invitations

Obviously, the invitation should be Humpty Dumpty. For each invitation:

1. Use an unlined white 3" x 5" index card and cut off the corners to form an oval (see fig. 1).

2. Use red construction paper for the bow tie. Fold construction paper in half the long way. Cut out two pieces for each bow tie as shown in fig 2.

fig. 1

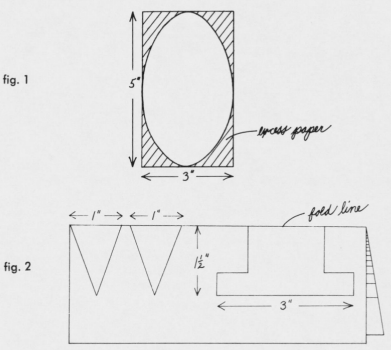

excess paper

fig. 2

fold line

3. Humpty's hat can also be made from red construction paper. Be sure to cut on fold line (see fig. 2).
4. Slip hat on top and glue in place. Glue the two pieces for the bow tie to the white oval so points meet at center and folds are on either side. Bow tie should open from center (see fig. 3).
5. Draw facial features as shown in fig. 3, and draw some cracks in lightly.

fig. 3

red construction paper

6. On hat write "RSVP" by (date and telephone number).

7. Before opening, write on left side of bow tie: Come Help Humpty Dumpty. On the right side write: Get it All Together Again.
8. Open both sides of the bow tie and on the left inside write:
    DATE: (day and date)
    TIME: (time and if for a meal)
    On the right side write:
    PLACE: (address)
    GIVEN BY: (name)

Decorations

Write simple nursery rhymes on sheets of paper (either white or colored) and hang them up around the room. Try to use rhymes that can be acted out by the children later on. There is no particular color scheme that relates to this party, so hang streamers and balloons in a variety of colors around the party room. You can draw Humpty Dumpty faces on the balloons first.

Humpty Dumpty should preside. You can make a Humpty Dumpty by using an old white pillowcase. Lay it flat and cut it into an oval in the same manner as the invitation. Put right sides together and sew a seam around it, leaving an opening to insert the stuffing. After stuffing the case, sew opening. Draw on a face and use a large scarf tied into a bow as the bow tie. Top with an old hat. Place him where he can watch all the activities.

Favors

The guests can be the King's men who try to put Humpty together again.

1. To make King's hats, use construction paper in any color. Fold in half the long way and cut as shown in fig. 4.

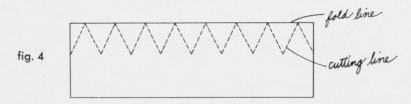

fig. 4

2. Tape the two pieces together to form a circle, using the head of the birthday child as a guide for size.
3. Write each child's name on a hat and put one on the table at each place.

"All the King's horses and all the King's men, couldn't put Humpty together again." A Put-Together Puzzle makes a good favor for the children to take home.

Put-Together Puzzle

1 greeting card (front picture)
   tongue depressors or popsicle sticks
   glue

Lay one tongue depressor or popsicle stick along the top of the greeting card picture. (If the picture is wider than it is high, lay it across the side of the picture.) Draw a line across the picture at the bottom edge of the stick. Lift stick and align the upper edge of the stick with the line you just made. Draw another line at the bottom edge of the stick. Continue drawing lines across the card, using the stick as a guide until the whole picture is covered (see fig. 5).

fig. 5

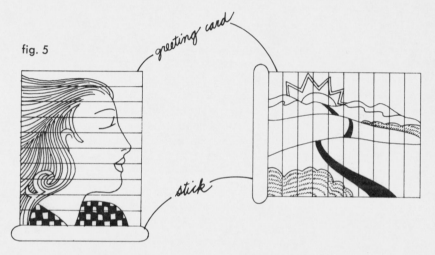

Cut the card into strips on the lines. Glue each strip to a stick. The children must lay the strips one beside the other to complete the puzzle. As an aid for the children, numbers can be written on the back of the sticks so they will be able to check on the proper order.

Food

Brick Wall Sandwich

2 slices white bread
2 slices square pumpernickel (Westphalian)
   egg salad

Make two egg salad sandwiches — one on white bread and one on pumpernickel. Cut each sandwich into four square pieces. Take two pieces of the white bread sandwich and two pieces of the pumpernickel sandwich and put them together on a plate to give a checkerboard effect (see fig. 6). Do the same with the other four sandwich pieces.

Yield: eight mini-sandwiches. Repeat if more are needed.

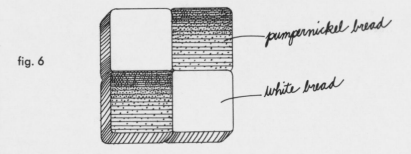

fig. 6

pumpernickel bread

white bread

King's Drink

Serve milk in a paper hot cup with a handle and write "KING" on the cup.

Humpty Dumpty Cake

1 package cake mix, any flavor
    (second box cake mix optional)
1 can ready-made vanilla frosting
1 can ready-made chocolate frosting (optional)
2 chocolate-covered mints
1 gumdrop
1 tube cake decorating gel (brown)
    colored sprinkles

Prepare cake mix according to package directions, using a 9" x 13" pan. If you want Humpty to have a hat, prepare second box of cake mix, using two 9" square pans. Let cakes cool. Cut 9" x 13" cake into oval by cutting off the corners (see fig. 7).

fig. 7

fig. 8

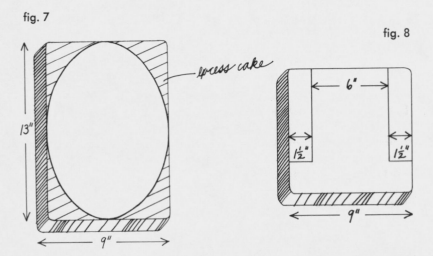

excess cake

13"

9"

6"

1½"

1½"

9"

For hat, cut 9" square cake as shown in fig. 8.

Frost oval cake with vanilla frosting. For hat, frost 9" cake with chocolate frosting. *IMPORTANT NOTE: If putting a hat on Humpty, be sure to cut off a piece from the top of the head and place hat on the cut edge. Decorate as in fig. 9.*

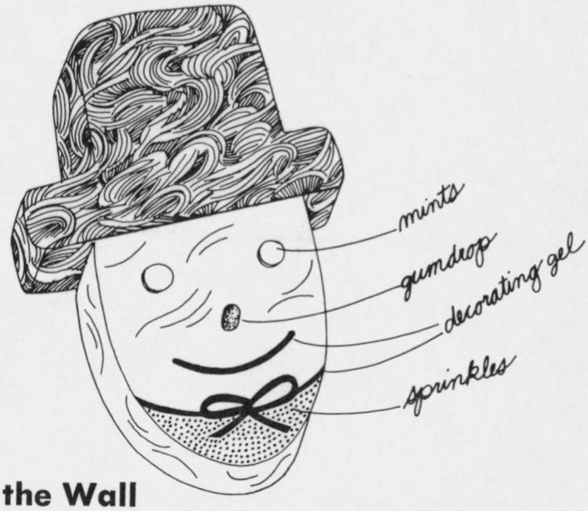

fig. 9

mints
gumdrop
decorating gel
sprinkles

Games

Pin Humpty on the Wall

Draw a picture of a wall on a piece of light-colored heavy paper. Cut white paper into egg shapes. Have the children draw Humpty Dumpty faces on the eggs. Hang up the picture of the wall. Attach masking tape to each Humpty Dumpty with a piece extending from the top. Blindfold one child at a time and face him or her in the direction of the wall. Let the child walk to the picture and stick Humpty on it. The one who sticks Humpty closest to the top of the wall is the winner.

Break Humpty Dumpty

Inflate balloons (one for each child) and draw Humpty's face on them. Attach a piece of string to each balloon. Tie a balloon to the ankle of each guest, with the balloon extending from the outside of the ankle. Have them take off their shoes and try to break each other's balloons while protecting their own. The last to have an unbroken balloon wins.

How Many Humpties Can Go Into a King's Hat?

Use thin cardboard to make a crown as done for the King's Hat. Cover the crown with aluminum foil. Place the crown on a throne (chair). Have the children line up a few feet from the throne and, one at a time, let them try to toss a plastic foam egg into the crown. There might be no winners or many winners in this game.

Special Activity

1. An older person can read the nursery rhymes on the wall and have the children act them out.
2. A group of people, whether they be older brothers or sisters or friends, can put on a play relating to nursery rhymes.

RAGTIME PARTY

Children enjoy rag dolls, and they get a lot of pleasure from playing house and having tea parties.

Invitations

You can make the invitations to a pretend tea party look like a rag doll's trousers. For each invitation:

1. Use blue construction paper and cut to 4" x 7". Fold in half to form Fold 1 (see fig. 1) and fold again on Fold 2 with the fold on your right. Cut a right triangle off the right corner and open Fold 2 (see fig. 1).

fig. 1

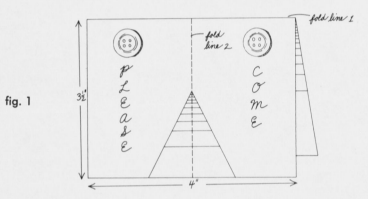

2. On outside glue two buttons and write "PLEASE" down the left leg and "COME" down the right leg (see fig. 1).
3. Open up the invitation and write the following:

OWNER OF THESE RAG DOLL PANTS: (name)

I LIVE AT: (address)

(On left leg write:)

PLEASE COME AT:

(time and meal)

(On right leg write:)

DATE:

(day and date)

4. Write the RSVP information on the inside of the front.

Decorations

The party room can be decorated with dolls. You can hang them on the walls or sit them on tables all around the room. Hang streamers from the ceiling and from the dolls for extra color. Blow up brightly colored balloons (at least one for each guest) and hang them around the room.

A clever touch would be to make rag doll faces on the balloons and hang streamers down the sides of the balloons to look like hair. Hang one of these rag doll balloons over the center of the table from a streamer.

Favors

The guests can become pretend rag dolls by wearing hats that make them look like dolls. For each hat:

1. Use a 7" white paper cake plate and punch holes around ¼ of the edge. These holes will be used for red yarn bangs. Punch two holes opposite each other for hat strings (see fig. 2).

fig. 2

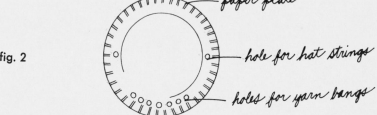

paper plate

hole for hat strings

holes for yarn bangs

2. Cut red yard into 6" pieces, one piece for each hole along the front edge. Fold each piece of yarn in half to form a loop and put the loop through a hole. Pull the ends through the loop and pull the ends gently but firmly to form a fringe. Repeat along the holes in the front edge to form bangs (omitting the holes for the hat strings).

3. Cut two pieces of yarn for hat strings, using the birthday child's head as a guide for the length of the strings. Attach these strings to the holes on either side with a knot. When putting the hats on the children, make sure the strings are behind their ears.

Since the theme of this party is related to rag dolls, a Dancing Doll is an appropriate favor, small and easy for children to handle.

Dancing Doll

    cardboard
    yarn
1½" plastic foam ball
   3 beads with holes in the center (1" diameter)
  1 plastic lid from ready-made frosting
24" elastic string
   3 sequins
    small piece of red yarn

For each doll, cut a piece of cardboard 5" high and 3" wide. Wrap yarn thirty full times around the 5" height of the cardboard. Slip yarn off the cardboard and tie about ½" from the looped ends (gathering all the loops). Snip loops. These are the arms. Repeat to make legs. To make a pom-pom for the top of the head, you need a pom-pom maker. For this, cut a 1″ diameter circle from the middle of the plastic lid. Cut a 13½ foot piece of yarn and fold in half. Going through the middle of the ring, wrap the yarn around the plastic rim. Keep wrapping until the whole rim is well covered. Cut loops open around outer rim of the ring by slipping point of scissors between loops and ring. Using a 6″ piece of yarn, tie all the snipped pieces together in the center and slip out of the ring. Fluff up and trim to circle shape. To assemble, take the elastic string and place yarn legs in the middle of string, tying the elastic around them. String the three beads over the doubled elastic. Set the yarn arms on top of the beads and tie the elastic string into a knot around them. Make a hole through the plastic foam ball and string elastic through it. Separate fibers of the pom-pom and tie elastic around its center. Tie free ends together to form a loop on the top. Glue sequins on ball for eyes and nose, and glue small piece of red yarn for the mouth.

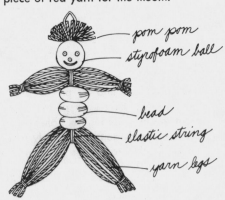

fig. 3

pom pom
styrofoam ball
bead
elastic string
yarn legs

Food

Raggetea Sandwiches

2 slices white bread per sandwich
  cream cheese

jelly
cookie cutters

Use cookie cutters to cut bread into different shapes. Make sure there are two pieces of bread of the same shape for each sandwich. Spread bread with cream cheese and jelly.

Rosy Cheeks Lemonade

Serve pink lemonade to go along with the food. Put two red maraschino cherries in the drink.

Happy Face Cake

1 package cake mix, any flavor
1 can ready-made frosting (cherry, strawberry or vanilla
      tinted pink with red food coloring)
  red string licorice
  chocolate-covered mints
3 maraschino cherries

Prepare cake mix according to package directions, using two 8″ or 9″ round cake pans. Let cake cool. Frost bottom cake layer and lay second cake layer on top. Frost entire cake and decorate as shown in fig. 4.

fig. 4

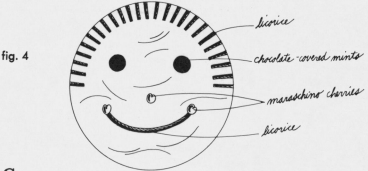

licorice

chocolate-covered mints

maraschino cherries

licorice

Games

Pass the Rag Doll

Have the guests sit in a circle and pass around a rag doll while someone claps. When the clapping stops, the child holding the rag doll leaves the circle. Play continues until there is one child left as the winner.

Pin the Pants on the Doll

Draw a picture of a doll (resembling a gingerbread man) on a large piece of paper or oak tag. Cut out the shape of pants to fit the doll (use pants shape on invitation as a guide). Hang picture on wall. Attach masking tape to pants with a piece extending from the top. Blindfold each child and face them one at a time in the direction of the doll picture. The one who comes the closest to getting the pants in the right place is the winner.

Special Activity

Use a roll of brown wrapping paper or any large paper and cut pieces the size of each child. If you cannot obtain the above paper, you can use one sheet of oak tag for each child. Stand the children in line and, one by one have them lie on a sheet of paper while you trace the child's outline in crayon. If you use oak tag, trace the child from the waist up. After all the outlines are completed, the guests can decorate their outlines and faces by gluing on such things as: fabric scraps, yarn, buttons, rickrack, lace or felt, turning their outlines into life-size dolls.

STRIKE UP THE BAND

How often have you enjoyed the sound of a good band? While the children may not make great sounds, they will very much enjoy being part of a birthday band.

Invitations

To carry out a band theme, the invitations can be shaped like band-leaders' hats.

1. Use colored construction paper to cut a 5″ x 5″ square for each invitation. Draw a line across each square 3″ from one edge (see fig. 1).

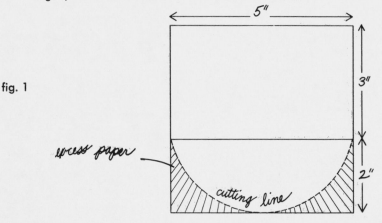

fig. 1

excess paper

cutting line

2. Draw a semicircle on the smaller portion of the rectangle from one end of the drawn line to the other. Cut out on semicircle line (see fig. 1).
3. To make a feather for the hat, use a piece of white paper 2″ x 3½″. Fold in half in the length and cut off corners to form a semicircle (see fig. 2).

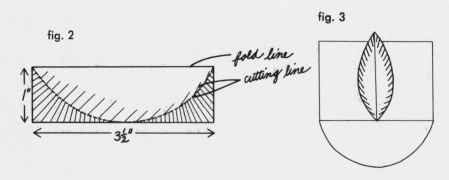

fig. 2

fig. 3

fold line

cutting line

4. Leaving paper folded, cut fringes on curved edge by snipping ½″ diagonal lines (see fig. 2).
5. Glue feather to hat with one point of feather resting on horizontal line and other point extending slightly above top edge (see fig. 3).
6. Write the birthday child's name on the feather.

7. The rest of the wording for the invitation can go on the visor of the hat, which can be folded up on the line for insertion into an envelope.

FOLLOW THE PARADE TO: (address)

BAND STARTS PLAYING AT: (time and if for meal)

ON: (day and date)

RSVP By   (date and phone number)

Decorations

Pictures of instruments and/or real instruments can be hung around the room. Records can be hung from the ceiling on streamers, or children's record covers can be hung on the walls. Aside from these decorations, draping twisted streamers from the ceiling and hanging balloons around the room will add still more flavor. The party favors, too, can be placed in some out-of-the-way spot in the room.

As a centerpiece you can make a drum from a round cookie tin or a two-pound coffee can (see the *Favors* section for directions). This drum can be used as a storage container for candy or little trinkets to give out as the children go home.

Favors

All the little bandleaders need hats, especially for the parade later on in the party.

1. Use 9″ x 12″ construction paper. Cut one sheet in half the long way (see fig. 4) for each hat.

fig. 4

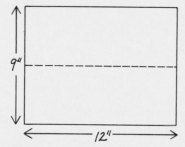

2. Lay the two strips end-to-end and tape together inside and out (see fig. 5).

fig. 5

3. Bring the two ends around and tape together to form a circle. Use the head of the birthday child as a guide for the size.

4. Trace a circle 7"-8½" in diameter onto construction paper and cut out. Cut the circle in half and use one-half as a visor for the hat.

5. Make a fold along the straight edge of the half-circle 1" from the edge (see fig. 6).

fig. 6

fig. 7

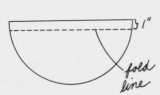

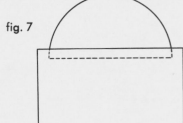

6. Tape the half-circle to the inside of the hat as shown in fig. 7, leaving the half-circle extending outward to form the visor of the hat.

7. The hat should have a feather for a decoration. You can purchase feathers or, if you live near a duck pond, you can find nice feathers to use. If you cannot find or buy feathers, you can make a paper feather as in the invitation, only larger to fit the hat.

Children love drums, and will enjoy taking a drum home with them.

Drum Holder/Bank

1 small peanut can with snap-on lid (3" high and
    3⅜" in diameter)
1 extra snap-on lid
  self-adhesive paper, any color
6 4" strips of ¾" wide adhesive cloth tape (or rickrack),
    contrasting color to paper
2 felt scraps large enough to cover three cotton balls
2 thin dowels, cut to 4¼" length
6 small cotton balls
2 pieces of yarn, 8" long
  glue
  scissors

Wash and dry can. If peanut cans are not available, use cardboard ready-made frosting cans and cut down to 3" height. Cut the adhesive paper 1" higher than the height of the can and wide enough to go around it. Cover the can with the paper and tuck the excess into the top of the can. Fasten the adhesive tape strips at diagonals onto the outside of the can, forming a zigzag design and overlapping the ends (if you use rickrack, glue it in the same fashion). Tuck the ends in on top and trim the ends on the bottom (see fig. 8).

Put lid on bottom and, in the center of the other lid, cut a 1" slot. Place lid on top. To make drumsticks, group three cotton balls together and

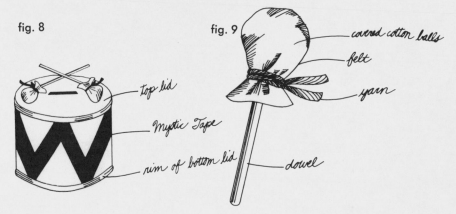

fig. 8

fig. 9

covered cotton balls

top lid

felt

Mystic Tape

yarn

rim of bottom lid

dowel

glue to top of one of the dowels. Wrap the cotton balls in a felt scrap, gathering the edges around the dowel. Wrap a piece of yarn around the gathered felt a few times and tie in a double knot. Trim the felt ends and the yarn (see fig. 9). Repeat this procedure for the other drumstick.

Lay the two drumsticks on top of the drum so the ends overlap. Tape the drumsticks to the lid where the sticks cross. The drum can be used to store candy, prizes or a few small crayons.

Food

Bandwiches

Serve hamburgers with two carrot sticks arranged like drumsticks on top of the bun.

Music Maker's Drink

Serve any flavor soft drink with the Bandwiches.

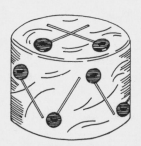

fig. 10

Lollipop Drum Cake

1 package prepared cake mix, any flavor
1 can ready-made frosting, any light color
   lollipops, large round

Prepare cake mix according to package directions, using two 8″ or 9″ round pans. Let cake cool. Frost one layer and put second layer on top. Frost entire cake. Press lollipops into sides of cake, forming a zigzag and having the stick of one lollipop meeting the candy end of the next (see fig. 10).

To make drumsticks, lay two lollipops on top of the cake with the sticks overlapping.

Games

The Big Parade

Children like to march around. Here is an opportunity to have a marching band. Give each child an instrument — they can be homemade or purchased. Here are some suggestions for making your own instruments:

A block and a spoon — hit together

A candy box — blow in the open end

A comb and a block — rub the comb on the edge of the block

Two cake or pie tins — hit together

Play marching music while the children march around a room playing their instruments.

Musical Pillows

Arrange pillows in a circle on the floor. Have one less pillow than the number of children. Stand the children in a circle inside the pillow circle. Play music while the children walk around the inside of the circle. When the music stops, everyone sits on a pillow. The one who is left without a pillow is out of the game. The music starts again, and the game continues until there is one child left. This is a good game for young children.

Pin the Drumsticks on the Drum

Draw a picture of a drum on a large piece of paper or oak tag. Put a circle in the middle of the top of the drum. Use pipe cleaners for drumsticks. Give each child a drumstick with a piece of masking tape across it. Blindfold each child and, one at a time, have them try to put the drumstick on the circle on top of the drum. The one who comes the closest is the winner.

Special Activity

Sing-along

If you know somone who plays an instrument, ask him or her to come to the party to help with the sing-along. Choose songs that the children should know. Otherwise, you can play records with familiar children's songs and have the guests sing along with the records.

Draw Your Favorite Instrument

Hang a long strip of brown wrapping paper across a wall. Be sure that, when the children reach up, the paper is high enough to cover their reaching height. You can use the birthday child as a guide. Draw vertical lines, dividing the paper into sections, one for each child. Write one name at the top of each section. Have each child draw with a crayon his favorite musical instrument in his section. Then have the children get up one at a time and point to their pictures and describe the instruments they drew and its sound. This paper can be kept by the birthday child as a memento or cut into sections and given to the children to take home.

CHAPTER III

Little Men's and Women's Birthday Parties (Ages 6-10)

The 6 to 10 age group is an easy group to work with. It seems no matter what you do with them, they are usually eager to go along and follow any directions given them. You can be very creative, and your party should be a great success if you plan carefully.

Children between 6 and 10 like being part of an "in-crowd." At a birthday party the children are not always from the same neighborhood or school and, therefore, are not all in the same "group." When the guests arrive at the party, make sure that introductions are made by the birthday child. If the party is for a fairly large group, preparing name tags is helpful. By involving all the children in a game as soon as they arrive, you bring the children together and keep them from separating into little groups.

Because some children in this age category tend to be a little boisterous, you must keep them busy at all times. If you prepare a party schedule, you will not be at a loss for what to do next. The children will go from one activity to another and will not have a chance to get out of hand.

Little men and women prefer not to wear party hats, so they can be dispensed with. Of course, they still enjoy all the other parts of a birthday party, particularly the cake.

As in the previous chapter, paper goods to go along with the colors or theme of the party should be used.

SUPERHEROES

Superheroes are in! They are known by all children. Little men and women often imagine themselves as one of these characters. A Superheroes party will give your guests a chance to live the part of their secret heroes.

Invitations

Some superheroes wear masks to disguise their identities. The invitations can be masks which will make a mystery of the kind of party you are giving until your guests arrive at the party.

1. Use colored construction paper and cut a 6″ x 7″ rectangle. Fold the paper in half, making a rectangle 3½″ x 6″ (see fig. 1).

fig. 1

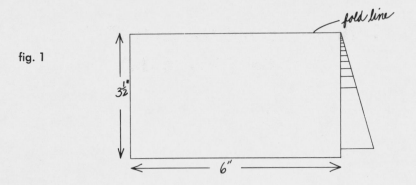

2. With the fold on top, round off the corners to form a mask as in fig. 2.

fig. 2

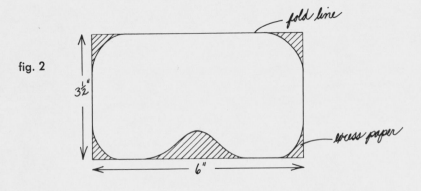

3. On the front piece, cut out two holes for eyes.
4. On outside of mask write: BIRTHDAY PARTY.
   Write the following in the eye holes so that when you open the card, the writing is on the inside:

                        (left eye hole)
                            FOR
                        (right eye hole)
              (NAME OF BIRTHDAY CHILD)

5. On inside:

              COME TO THE SECRET CAVE:
                        (address)
   DATE: (day and date)   TIME: (time and if for a meal)
   See fig. 3 for completed mask.

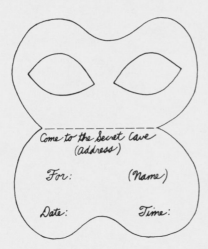

fig. 3

Come to the Secret Cave
(address)

For: *(Name)*

Date: *Time:*

Decorations

Some superheroes fly. You can make the ceiling of the party room resemble a sky. Use light blue streamers for the decorations. Hang a large yellow balloon on a streamer over the center of the table. This is the sun. Cut out cloud shapes from white paper and hang these from streamers all around the room. If you have any superhero dolls, you can tie one end of a streamer around the dolls' waist and hang the other end from the ceiling.

Use yellow balloons and cluster them in corners of the room. Be sure there are enough for everyone.

If you have pictures of superheroes, hang them on the walls. As a centerpiece, you can use a book or record and place it in the center of the table. If you have an extra doll, or if you do not wish to hang the dolls, you can use one or several for a centerpiece.

Favors

Something personal and also practical for a child's room is a waste-paper basket. Maybe it will encourage the children to keep their rooms tidy!

Here are the materials you will need for the Super-Tidy Basket:
1 2-lb. coffee can or any other container approximately this size
   red self-adhesive paper
1 sheet white construction paper
1 sheet blue construction paper
   scissors
   glue

Wash and dry can thoroughly. Cut a piece of red self-adhesive paper 1″ higher than the height of the can and wide enough to go around it. Cover the can with self-adhesive paper and tuck the excess into the top of the can. Fold the white construction paper in half and cut a rectangle as shown in fig. 4.

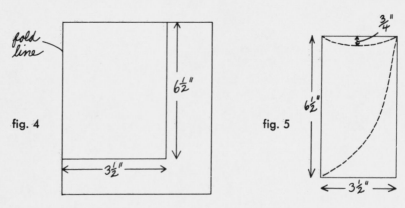

fig. 4

fig. 5

Leaving the paper folded, draw a small semicircle along the top of the paper from one corner to the other. The deepest point of the semicircle should be ¾″. From the bottom corner on the folded side, draw an arc extending upward to the opposite top corner (see fig. 5). Cut along lines. When completed and unfolded, the emblem should look like this:

fig. 6

Glue the emblem to the side of the can. With blue construction paper, cut out a block letter (child's first initial) and glue the letter to the center of the emblem.

Food

Super Hero Sandwich

Put two or three slices of luncheon meat on a miniature loaf of Italian bread or long Italian roll. Serve potato chips on the side. Mix mayonnaise, ketchup and a little relish to make a Russian dressing. Put it in a bowl on the table and call it the Secret Power Sauce.

Kryptonade

Serve orangeade with a green ice cube floating in each glass. The ice cube is made from green (citrus) punch frozen in an ice cube tray.

Cape Cake

1 package cake mix, any flavor
1 can ready-made frosting, chocolate
1 tube cake decorating gel, light color

Prepare cake mix according to package directions, using a 13" x 9" pan. Let cake cool. Cut cake and arrange according to fig. 7. Cut off the top point as shown with the dotted line.

fig. 7

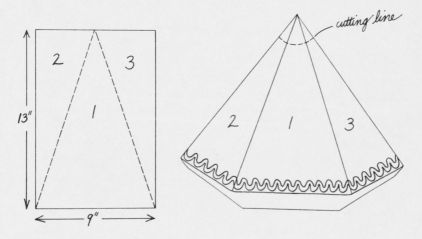

Cover cake with chocolate frosting and use the tube of gel to put the birthday child's first initial on it. You can also use the cake decorating gel to decorate the bottom edge of the cake with scallops as shown.

Games

Disguise Your Identity Game

For this game you will need two pairs of baggy pants, two baggy shirts and two pairs of gloves. Divide the children into two teams and have them line up behind some markers. These can be two chairs or two pieces of tape on the floor. Place markers opposite each of the two teams on the other side of the room. Put each of the two sets of clothes in a paper shopping bag, one for each team. The first child on each team puts the clothes on over his or her own clothes as fast as possible and runs to the other side of the room. There the child takes the clothes off, puts them into the bag and carries the bag of clothes to the next person on his or her team. The first team to finish is the winner.

Weaker and Stronger

This is a variation of the old favorite game of "Hot and Cold." Have one child leave the room. Have someone hide a rock (call it "Zargon") in the room while everyone watches. Have the person come back in the room and try to find the hiding place by moving around the room. If the child gets near the rock, everyone yells "getting weaker"; as he or she moves away, the child is "getting stronger." One has to be very weak to find the rock.

Special Activity

Super Placemats

Use one sheet of 9" x 12" construction paper for each child. Have each one draw his or her favorite superhero on the paper. If they are reluctant to draw one, you can have some pictures of superheroes available for them to glue onto the paper and decorate. Have each child write his or her name on the front of the picture. Cut out two pieces of clear self-adhesive paper 9" x 12" and stick one to each side of the finished artwork. This preserves the drawings and makes them suitable for use as a personalized placemat.

Have a Superhero Visit the Party

A costume can be made or rented and someone, either an adult or child, can dress us as a superhero and give out little trinkets, candy and the favors to the guests.

OUTTA SIGHT

From the days of Buck Rogers to the days of Artoo Detoo children have had a love affair with science fiction and outer space. The minds and imaginations of all youngsters are aroused by the stars, the planets, astronauts, and even creatures from space. Because science fiction is just that — fiction — your own creative imagination can ignite one of the best parties you'll give. "Blast off. . . ."

Invitations

It's time to take off for outer space. Make the invitation a space vehicle.

1. Cut a piece of colored construction paper in half across the width to form a rectangle.
2. Fold paper in half lengthwise to form a fold line. Open after making fold.

3. Hold the paper with the length on the sides and fold the two top corners down to meet at the center fold. With the top corners folded, close on the center fold line.
4. Fold each flap back and in half (see fig. 1).

fig. 1

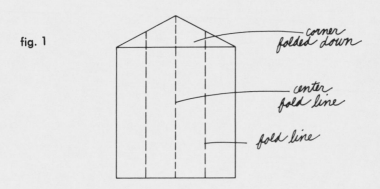

corner folded down

center fold line

fold line

5. The wording for the invitation can be written on the wings:

fig. 2

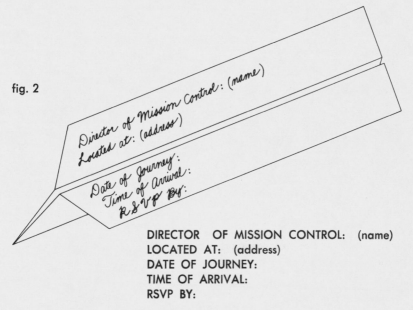

Director of Mission Control: (name)
Located at: (address)

Date of Journey:
Time of Arrival:
R S V P By:

DIRECTOR OF MISSION CONTROL: (name)
LOCATED AT: (address)
DATE OF JOURNEY:
TIME OF ARRIVAL:
RSVP BY:

Decorations

Make stars from cardboard and cover with aluminum foil. Hang the stars from streamers over the party table. Use a globe as a centerpiece if you have one.

Favors

Children in this age group begin to learn the value of money. They like to save it and watch it mount up. The favor for this party can be a Spaceship Bank which the children can make themselves. You will need the following materials:

1 Pringle's Potato Chip® can, or any other cardboard
     can that size with a lid, for each favor
  yarn, any color
  glue
  small party hat, 4" diameter opening
  oak tag or colored cardboard
  white self-adhesive paper
  scissors

Before the party, a bag should be made up for each child with all of the prepared items needed to make the favor.

Wash and dry can. Cut two vertical slits 2¾" on either side of the can, going from the bottom up. From the oak tag paper, cut a trapezoid as in fig. 3.

fig. 3

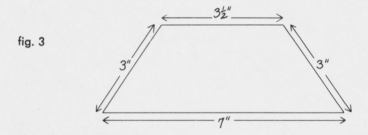

The ladder and door of the spaceship are made from the white self-adhesive paper. Cut a rectangle 5¼" x 1¾" and cut out rectangular holes to make the piece appear like a ladder. For the door, cut a piece of self-adhesive paper 1¾" wide and 1¾" high. On one side, make an arch shape for the top of the door. Cut a 1" slot in the center of the lid of the can. Make a small ball of yarn for each child and place in a small bag with the pieces you just prepared. At the time of the party, give each child a bag along with some glue on a piece of paper. They can use either inexpensive paint brushes or their fingers to spread the glue around the can, starting at either the top or the bottom, working 1" at a time. Holding the end of the yard at the edge, the children should wrap the yarn around the can as close together as possible, working their way down the can until it is completely covered. Cut through the yarn where the slits were previously made (do not let the children do this). Slide the oak tag trapezoid through the can so that a triangle protrudes on either side (if you have trouble getting it through, use a metal spatula to guide it). Bend the triangles forward a little.

Have each child remove the backing on the ladder and stick it on the side of the can between the cardboard tail fins. Remove the backing on the door and stick it above the ladder. Use the point of a pair of scissors to push a hole through the side of the can 1″ from the top. Detach the elastic on one side of the hat and push end through the hole in the can and tie a knot on the inside (do the last two operations yourself). Have the children put the lids on the can and place hats on top to form nose cones (see fig. 4).

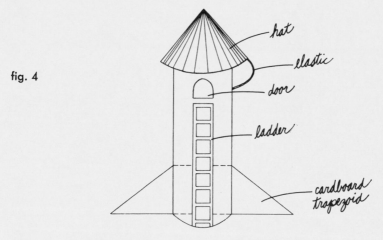

fig. 4

- hat
- elastic
- door
- ladder
- cardboard trapezoid

Food

Cheese Rocket Sandwiches

Prepare enough grilled cheese sandwiches to yield 1¼ per child. Put sandwich together to look like a rocket ship, using cheese triangles as fins (see fig. 5).

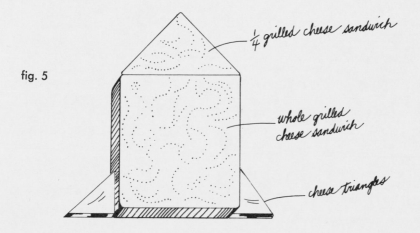

fig. 5

- ¼ grilled cheese sandwich
- whole grilled cheese sandwich
- cheese triangles

Milky Way Drink

Prepare chocolate milk and float miniature marshmallows in it.

Sunshine Cake

1 box prepared cake mix, any flavor
1 can ready-made frosting, lemon or vanilla tinted yellow
 pretzel rods broken in half, or pretzel logs
Prepare cake mix according to package directions, using two 8" or 9" round pans. Let cakes cool. Frost as for a two-layer cake. Lay pretzel rods around cake and ½" away from cake to look like sun rays (see fig. 6).

fig. 6

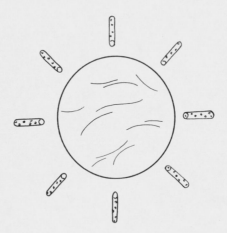

Games

Space-O

Make up a 5" x 5" cardboard or oak tag card for each child. Draw twenty-five 1" squares. Write a word related to space in each of the twenty-five squares on each card. Use the same words, but switch their order on all cards. On some cards use a few words that do not appear on the following list. Write each of the words on a small piece of paper. Put the papers in a bag. Gather a supply of small buttons.

Give out one card to each child along with some buttons and have the birthday child pick out one slip of paper at a time from the bag and call out a word. As the word is called, each child who has the word on his card puts a button on it. The first child to cover all squares on the outer edge wins and yells "Space-O."

Suggested words are:

Mercury	Launch	Orbit	Earth
Venus	Nose Cone	Reentry	Sun
Neptune	Mars	Retrorocket	Meteors
Saturn	Stars	Tail Fin	Asteroids
Comets	Moon	Uranus	Space Man
Gravity	Pluto	Jupiter	Solar System

Flying Saucer Game

Make flying saucers by stapling or taping tart-size aluminum tins together. Hang a swimming tube or a plastic foam ring in a doorway. Have the children form a line behind a marker placed on the floor (distance depends on age) and try to toss flying saucers through the ring. If time permits, give the children more than one turn. To add difficulty to the game, you can make the ring swing a little and give the children a moving target.

Special Activity

Moonhunt

For this activity, you will need a separate room with a door. On the door, hang a sign saying, "Walk on the Moon." Put pillows or other soft items around the middle of the floor. Cover everything with a large white sheet or blanket. Blow up enough balloons for everyone and attach strings to each. Write the name of a planet on a sticker for each balloon. Stick the planet names on the balloons (you might have to repeat some names if you have a larger number of children). Hang the balloons by the strings from the ceiling, being sure they are low enough to touch the children's heads. Wrap pennies in aluminum foil, allowing a certain number per child, and put the wrapped pennies on the sheet or blanket in all the creases. Darken the room, have the children remove shoes and line up. Let them jump from one crater to the next (pillow-to-pillow) while hunting for stars (wrapped pennies). Allow six children in the room at one time. If they fall off, they have to start over. Give a limit to the number of stars each child is allowed. When they reach the limit they must leave the moon. When the children are ready to go home, they may go back to the moon and take a planet (balloon).

FUN FAIR

The smiles are broad and the laughs are loud when children attend a carnival or fun fair. From the food to the rides and the games, a fun fair is one of the greatest thrills in a youngster's life, no matter what his age. Your own home can instantly become a fair with a little effort.

Invitations

Fun fairs use tickets for admissions and prizes. Your invitation can look like a ticket, too.
1. Use an unlined 3″ x 5″ index card and cut out a semicircle on each 3″ side (see fig. 1).

fig. 1

2. Write:

ADMIT ONE
TO A BIRTHDAY PARTY
TO: (name)'s House
        (address)
DATE: (day and date)
TIME: (time and if for a meal)
RSVP BY:

Decorations

The decorations for this party will be the games placed all around a room or outside in a yard. There will be six games and a balloon booth with colorful balloons.

Favors

Tic Tac Tote

For each favor:
2 pieces felt 8" x 9"
2 snaps
  scissors
  glue
  needle and thread
  rickrack
  yarn (optional)
10 poker chips — 5 each of two colors

Cut four 9" pieces of rickrack. Glue onto one piece of felt to form tic tac toe design with 2½" squares. Put the two pieces of felt wrong sides together, being sure to tuck in ½" excess rickrack on three sides. Pin in place. Bend in 8" side ½" to form hem. Pin in place. Sew three sides together, omitting hem side. Sew hem. Fasten two snaps to opening on inside. If favor is for a girl, it can be made into a pocketbook by sewing on a braided handle made out of yarn. This favor can be used as a traveling game. For the x's and o's, use two different color poker chips (ten in all), place in a plastic bag and put in the pouch.

Food

Lucky Dogs
Serve frankfurters on buns and French fries.

Fun Drink
Fill a glass half-full with your favorite flavor soda. Add one scoop any flavor ice cream and stir gently.

Bull's Eye Cake
1 package cake mix, any flavor
2 cans ready-made frosting (1 vanilla & 1 chocolate)
2 tubes cake decorating gel (1 brown and 1 white)
Prepare cake mix according to package directions, using two 9" round pans. Let cakes cool. Frost bottom layer with chocolate frosting on the top of the layer and then on the sides. Place other cake layer on top. On top of cake, mark off circles for target by using the lid of a 2-lb. coffee can. Lay the lid on top of the cake in the center and press lightly to make a circle. Use a cup or glass with a 2" diameter circle and center it within the other circle. Press down to mark off. Frost center circle with vanilla. Frost next ring with chocolate and frost outer ring with vanilla. After top is frosted, complete the frosting on the sides of the cake with the chocolate frosting. On the center circle, write the birthday child's age with brown tube of decorating gel. On the next ring, write a lower number than the age in white and on outer ring, write a still lower number in brown. The cake should look like this:

fig. 2

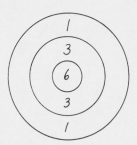

Games and Special Activity

The games for this party can be set up around a room, or outdoors in a yard. Since there are seven booths for the Fun Fair and they will take a good amount of time, we have combined them with the Special Activity.

Before the Fun Fair, prepare tickets by cutting 3" x 5" index cards in half and having the birthday child decorate them. As a child wins a game, give him or her a ticket.

To keep everything under control during the Fun Fair, have the children form a line at the first booth. After this game is done by everyone, the line can move on to the next booth. This way, if you don't have help, you can supervise each game and give out the tickets. After all the games have been played, the one with the most tickets is the winner of the Fun Fair. Here is a list of the booths and the directions for preparing each:

Bull's Eye Game

2 pieces of oak tag   scissors
3 2" plastic foam balls   ruler
  tape or glue

Using oak tag paper, measure strips 5" high across the entire width. You will be making three rings for the target from these 5" high strips. The largest one is 5" high and 51" long (allow an extra 4" for overlapping when taping together), the middle ring is 5" high and 30" long (allow 4" for overlap when taping together) and the smallest ring is 5" high and 11½" long (allow an extra 4" for overlapping). Tape the ends of each ring together and place on a piece of oak tag 22" x 22", centering each ring within the other on the oak tag. Tape or glue the rings in place.

Have the children stand in line, one behind the other, a few feet from the game. Give the first one in line three plastic foam balls and let him or her toss them, one at a time, into the target, trying to get the ball in the center. The ones who get it in the center receive a ticket.

Tic Tac Toe

24" x 24" piece of plywood or any other thin wood
1½" wide adhesive cloth tape
5 poker chips
  ruler
  scissors

Using the piece of plywood, mark off a 7" line parallel to one edge and lay a strip of tape across the board at this marking, leaving the 7" space between the edge of the board and the edge of the tape. Mark a 7" line parallel to the opposite edge and lay a strip of cloth tape across that line, leaving the 7" space between the tape and the edge. Do the same thing on the other two edges to complete the board.

Have everyone form a line a few feet from the board which is placed on the floor. The first one in line takes the poker chips and tries to toss the chips to make tic tac toe in any direction. The ones who get tic tac toe receive a ticket.

Ring the Pencils

6 unsharpened pencils   glue
1 cardboard ready-made frosting can   scissors
1 cardboard gift box (about 10" x 12")

Push the pencils through the top of the closed gift box, making three rows — one in the front, two in the middle row and three in the back row. Leave 3" between each pencil and make rows 3" apart. To secure the pencils, put glue on the unsharpened ends and push them in the box until the end touches the bottom of the box. Cut the frosting can into three rings (1" wide), discarding the bottom.

Have everyone form a line a few feet from the box, which is placed on the floor or on a table. Give the first one in line three rings. The object of the game is to get a ring on a pencil. Give one ticket for each pencil they ring.

Buttons Down

6 baby food jars (without lids)
4 ¾" buttons

Set up the baby jars as in the Ring the Pencils game — one in the front, two in the middle and three in the back row. Be sure all the jars are touching each other.

Have everyone form a line and give four buttons to the first one in line. The object of the game is to toss the buttons into the jar. Give one ticket for each button that lands in a jar.

Knock Down the Cans

6 cans from tennis balls or Pringle's Potato Chips®
    (or a combination of both)
2 pairs socks rolled into two balls

Set up cans in three rows — three in the back row, two in the middle and one in the front — leaving about 2" between cans.

Have everyone form a line, giving the first one in line the two balls. Each person has two chances to get a strike (knock all the cans down). Give a ticket to each child who gets a strike.

Lollipop Cone

Purchase a plastic foam cone 12" high. Put marks on the bottom of some of the lollipop sticks. Push the sticks into the plastic foam. Give each child a chance to take a lollipop from the cone. If there is a mark on the stick, they keep the lollipop. This is a nice booth to have near the end of the fair since there is no score involved and they can eat the lollipops. (You can even cheat a little and put marks on *all* the sticks).

Balloon Booth

Inflate enough balloons for everyone and put a guest's initial on each balloon. Attach each balloon to a thin dowel stick.

Set up a small table and on it place a round piece of styrofoam with all the balloons stuck in it.

WILD WEST

East or west, north or south, children all over the continent look back at the heroes and legends of the old Wild West. Cowboys, cowgirls and Indians are as much a part of growing up as running noses and belly-aches. The latter two do not make a good party theme, but the former ones do, "pardner."

Invitations

Since lassos were an essential part of a cowpoke's equipment, they make a unique and suitable design for an invitation.

1. Fold a piece of colored construction paper in half lengthwise and then cut in half (see fig. 1).

fig. 1

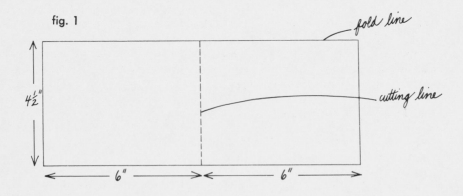

2. Using a piece of yarn, make a large loop with a knot and glue on front of the card to look like a lasso (see fig. 2).
3. On outside, in loop, write: Howdy, Pardner.
   On inside, write:

fig. 2

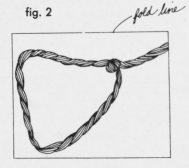

Come to (name)'s Covered Wagon

AT: (address)

ON: (date)

CHOW TIME: (time and if for a meal)

RSVP BY:

When the guests respond, be sure to ask the mothers for permission to take the children on pony rides.

Decorations

For a Wild West atmosphere, you can hang things relating to cowboys, cowgirls and Indians on the walls. Some suggestions are: a rope shaped like a lasso, six-shooter guns, toy horses and pictures of cowboys, cowgirls and Indians. Hang a WANTED poster for each child, with a drawing of the child and the child's name beneath.

You can create a tepee effect over the party table by hanging streamers from the ceiling above the center of the table to each corner of the table. Tape the ends of the streamers to the corners. The streamers will look a little more decorative if you hold one streamer horizontally and place the end of another streamer on top vertically as shown in fig. 3 and tape in place.

fig. 3

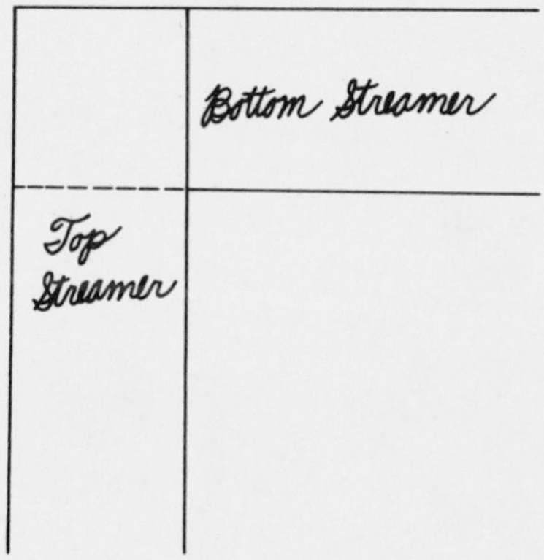

Holding the horizontal piece, fold it to the left over the vertical piece. Now take the vertical streamer and bring it up and across the other streamer. Continue doing this until the streamer is the desired length. Be sure to keep untangling the streamer ends as you go along.

Favors

Children in this age group enjoy writing notes to their friends. You can give them some special pencils as a memento of your Wild West party.

Arrows in a Quiver
4" fringe trim from sewing notions store
2 pencils (about 7½")
2 pieces felt 5" x 2"
1 tube ball-point paint or tube of glitter
  scissors
  needle and thread

Cut fringe into four 1'' pieces. Glue one piece to either side of the eraser end of a pencil to look like feathers on the end of an arrow. Do the same with the other pencil. Sharpen pencils. To make a quiver for the arrows, put the two pieces of felt together and stitch a ¼'' seam around three sides of felt, leaving the 2'' side open. If you have pinking shears, pink the edges, being careful not to snip the stitching. Write each child's first name with ball-point paint or glitter down the front of the quiver. Put pencils in the quiver with the points down and the feather end sticking out.

Food

Cowburger
Serve hamburgers on buns with baked beans.

Cactus Juice
Serve lemon and lime soft drink with a splash of maraschino cherry juice and a cherry.

Teepee Cake
1 package cake mix, any flavor
1 can ready-made frosting (milk chocolate)
    pretzel logs
1 tube cake decorating gel (white or yellow)
Prepare cake mix according to package directions, using a 13'' x 9'' pan. Let cake cool. Cut out cake as shown in fig. 4.

fig. 4

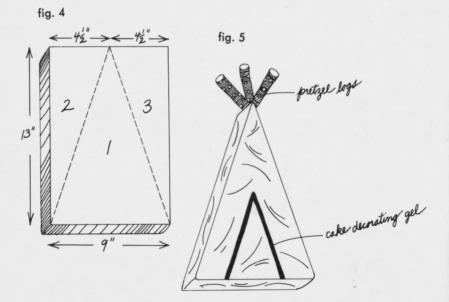

fig. 5

Take pieces #2 and #3 and lay together to form a triangle under piece #1. Be sure to frost over pieces #2 and #3 before laying piece #1 on top. Frost entire cake. Decorate as in fig. 5.

Games

Cowpoke and Indian Wrestle

Set up two chairs at a small table. Have the children form a line. To arm wrestle, two people sit opposite one another at the table with their right elbows on the table and right hands clasped together. Each one tries to push the other's arm over while keeping elbows on the table. The winner stays seated and the next one in line arm wrestles with him. Begin with the first two people and continue until everyone has had a turn.

Rope the Hat

From a heavy piece of rope, make a loop large enough to go over a Western-style hat. Lay the hat on the floor and have everyone form a line opposite the hat a number of feet away (exact distance depends on the age of the children). Have each child try to drop the lasso around the brim of the hat. The one who does is the winner.

Special Activity

Pony Rides

You can take the cowpokes and Indians on pony rides for a special treat. Even in the big cities, there are stables.

Before you leave for the pony rides, prepare a bag containing numbered slips of paper. Let each child pick a number to determine his or her turn. After some children have had their turns riding the ponies, you can take them aside and play a game to keep them busy until everyone is finished.

Balloon Cowpoke

Inflate enough balloons for everyone and attach to thin dowels. Have each child draw a face on a balloon with a felt-tip pen, and give each one a bandanna to tie around the dowel right below the balloon. The children can each draw the outline of a Western-style hat on construction paper and cut it out. Stick the hat to the balloon with tape above the face.

If you take the children on pony rides, the balloons can be decorated ahead of time and hung around the room.

LET'S PLAY BALL

Super Bowl, World Series, Stanley Cup, basketball, soccer . . . sports, sports, sports. This is a world of sports and a sure bet theme for a party for boys, girls or both.

Invitations

Since this party is a sports party, the invitation should resemble a ball.
1. Use yellow, white or orange construction paper and fold in half lengthwise.
2. Use the top of a ½-pound margarine tub as a pattern for a 4″ diameter circle and draw the circle with a segment of it on the fold (see fig. 1).

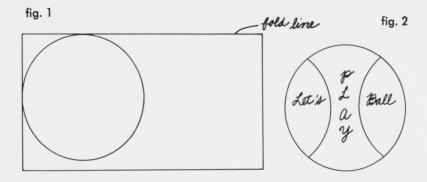

fig. 1   — fold line   fig. 2

3. Cut out the circle, leaving a piece attached at the fold.
4. On the outside, draw lines as in fig. 2 and print "LET'S PLAY BALL" as shown.
5. Open up the invitation and write the following:

Come Join the Birthday Fun!

STADIUM LOCATION: (address)

GAME DATE: (day and date)

GAME TIME: (time and if for a meal)

COACH: (name)

RSVP BY: (date and telephone number)

Decorations

If you have a ping pong table, cover it with a tablecloth, leaving the net on and in the center. If you don't have a ping pong table, a piece of cardboard with lines drawn on it to resemble a net can be attached to your party table.

Hang pictures of athletes and pictures of people participating in sports on the walls (baseball or any other sports cards can be used). Decorate the room with hats, sticks, or bats, balls from all types of sports, or even the sports section of the newspaper.

Inflate enough balloons for everyone and draw lines on them using the lines on the invitation as a guide. Attach string to the balloons and group them over the center of the table.

Favors

With a Baseball Mitt Washcloth as a party favor, children will stay in the bathtub longer and might come out cleaner, too!

Baseball Mitt Washcloth

fig. 3

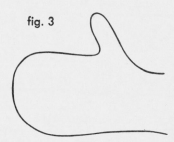

terry cloth
needle and thread
scissors
elastic (¼" wide)
cardboard

Make a pattern for the mitt on cardboard, using your hand as a guide. When outlining your hand, have your thumb out to the side and your other four fingers together. Don't outline each finger, just round off the top of the mitt as in fig. 3.

Cut out the cardboard on the outline and trace onto two pieces of terry-cloth. Cut out the two pieces and pin together. Sew a ¼" seam around the mitt leaving the bottom open. Fold down to a ½" hem towards outside and sew as close to the edge of the fabric as possible, leaving a small opening to insert elastic. Cut a piece of elastic 1" longer than the width of the birthday child's hand. Using a safety pin attached to one end of the elastic, push it through the hem at the opening, being sure the other end does not slip into the hem. Sew the two ends of the elastic together, overlapping them a little. Close up the hem opening. Turn the mitt right-side-out. If small round guest soap is available, give one out with each mitt. A small sports picture can be glued to the soap and then glazed with découpage glaze on the picture side of the soap only.

Food

Bologna Ball Sandwich

mustard in squeeze container with tip
2 slices bologna
1 hamburger bun

Put the two slices of bologna in the hamburger bun. On top of the bun make lines as in fig. 4. If the children find it a little messy to eat, they can turn the top over so the mustard is inside the sandwich.

Champion's Drink

Serve Gatorade thirst quencher, the drink of athletes, with the sandwiches.

Fork Ball (a baseball pitch)

1 package cake mix, any flavor
1 can ready-made frosting (vanilla)
1 tube brown cake decorating gel

Prepare cake mix according to package directions, using a 2-quart round glass casserole or two 8″ or 9″ round pans. If baking cake in the glass casserole, allow extra baking time and test cake as directed on package. Let cake cool. Frost 8″ or 9″ cakes to make a two-layer cake. If you use the glass casserole, frost the entire cake. With a toothpick, mark lines on the frosting as in the invitation. Using these lines as a guide, make v's on them to look like the stitching on the ball.

Games

Strainer Catch

Have the children form two lines facing each other. The first person on each side is given a medium-sized strainer with a handle. Give one of the first two players a tennis ball. The person with the ball starts the game. He or she must toss the ball to the person opposite him, using the strainer to toss it; the other person must catch the ball in the strainer. A contestant who misses is out, and the next one in line gets the strainer. If this player doesn't miss, he or she remains in line and passes the strainer to the next one. Play continues passing the strainer down the line on both sides with the people missing the ball leaving the line. After everyone has had a turn, the team with the most players left is the winning team. If the teams tie, you can play another round.

Baseball Miniature Golf

This game can be played either indoors or out. Set up four holes in the form of a baseball diamond. The starting hole is on First Base, then proceed to Second Base, Third Base and Home Base. To play the game, all you need is a golf ball or any other ball that size. The object of the game is to roll the ball through the obstacles and into each hole with the least amount of rolls. After each roll, the ball is picked up and rolled from the point where it stopped. To make the game a little more realistic, you can prepare a score card with the four holes listed and the name of each child down the side. You can then fill in the number of tries it takes each player to get the ball into each of the four holes.

fig. 4

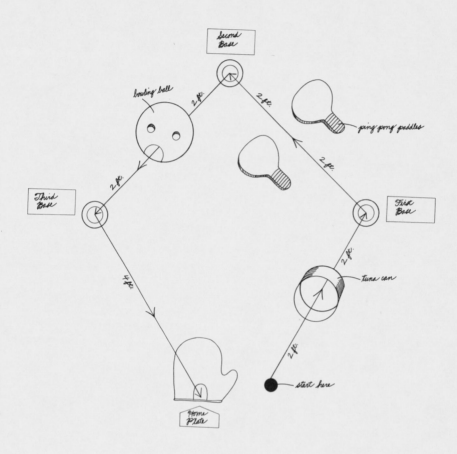

Second Base

bowling ball

2 ft.

2 ft.

ping pong paddles

2 ft.

Third Base

2 ft.

First Base

2 ft.

tuna can

4 ft.

2 ft.

start here

Home Plate

FIRST BASE — Basketball Hoop

Remove label, top and bottom of a 6½ oz. tuna can. Wash and dry thoroughly.

To set up the first hole, lay the can on its side and tape it to the floor. Trim off the rolled edge of an aluminum pie plate so that the slanted side of the pan is smooth. Cut a 3½" hole in the bottom of the plate. Lay the inverted plate 2 feet from the tuna can.

SECOND BASE — Ping Pong

Use two ping pong or other kind of paddle. Lay the paddles on the floor and tape them 5" apart. Lay an inverted aluminum pie plate (cut as above) two feet from the paddles. The children must try to roll the ball between the two paddles and into the hole. If the ball touches a paddle, there is a one-stroke penalty.

THIRD BASE — Bowling Base

Cut a 9" circle from black cardboard or paint a 9" cardboard circle black. Draw three white holes on the cardboard to resemble a bowling ball. One hole should be on the bottom edge (cut this hole out) and the other two above it. Use a half-gallon milk container with the top cut off as a support for the circle. On two opposite sides of the container cut out holes 2" high from the bottom and ½" in from either side. Paste the bowling ball to the side of the container with the cut out hole of the ball on the bottom, matching up with one of the holes in the container. Lay an inverted aluminum pie plate 2 feet from the back of the bowling ball.

HOME PLATE — Baseball Mitt

Cut a baseball mitt shape out of brown oak tag or cardboard painted brown. Cut a hole at the bottom for a golf ball to go through.

Use a half-gallon milk container with the top cut off as a support for the mitt. On one side of the container at the bottom, cut out a hole 2" high and ½" in from either side. Paste the mitt to the side of the container with the holes matching up. See the preceding diagram for the layout of the game.

Special Activity

Baseball Piñata

1½ cups flour
1¼ cups water
   newspaper strips
1 round balloon (at least 6" in diameter)
   white poster paint
   black poster paint
   paint brush
   string

Mix flour and water together to form a thick paste. Rest the knotted end of an inflated balloon on a glass with a large top. Dip strips of newspaper into the paste one at a time, wiping off excess paste on the edge of the bowl. Lay the strips on the balloon, overlapping them as you do so. Continue to dip the strips in the paste and lay them on the balloon until the whole balloon is well covered with a thin layer of paper strips. Leave the knot of the balloon exposed. Gently smooth out the paper-covered balloon with your fingers. Let it sit until dry (it could take two days). When the paper is dry, cut the balloon near the knot and pull it out. Make sure the hole in the ball is about 2" wide. If it is smaller, you can use a small scissors or a razor blade to make it a little larger. Paint the ball white and paint black lines on it to make it look like a baseball.

After the paint is dry, you can fill the ball with small trinkets such as toy charms, pennies, small candies or balloons in measured amounts for each child. Punch two holes for string on either side of the hole on top of the ball. Run a string through the two holes and use the string for hanging.

Hang the piñata from the ceiling or an entranceway. Have the children sit in a circle around the area. Give the birthday child the honor of trying to break the piñata. Blindfold the child and give him or her a plastic baseball bat. Tell the child to hit the piñata and try to break it open. If the children are older, you can swing the piñata a little to make it more difficult. When it breaks, all the children can pick up the trinkets from the floor. Put a limit on the number of items each can take, thus making it fair for everyone.

If weather permits and you have the outdoor area, you can organize an athletic game such as baseball, basketball, soccer, football, etc. If you plan on doing this, make a note on your invitations suggesting that the children wear play clothes to the party.

MOVIES AT HOME

Children enjoy going to the movies or watching movies and/or cartoons on TV. Instead of taking your party to the movies, have the movies at your party.

Invitations

You can design your invitation like a movie theater marquee.
1. Use 9" x 12" construction paper and fold in half lengthwise.
2. Cut the folded paper in half to form two folded rectangles 6" x 4½" (see fig. 1).

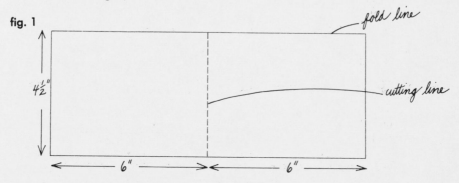

fig. 1

fold line

cutting line

4½"

6"   6"

3. On the front piece, measure a 1" border all around and cut out a rectangle in the middle.
4. Print "MOVIES AT HOME" on the outside top and draw circles around the border to resemble marquee lights. See fig. 2 for the rest of the wording.

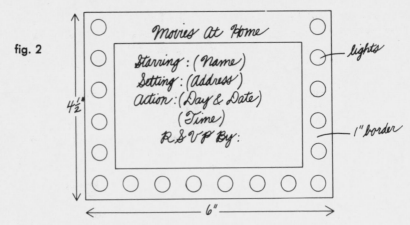

fig. 2

Movies At Home

Starring: (Name)
Setting: (Address)
Action: (Day & Date)
(Time)
R.S.V.P. By:

lights

1" border

4½"

6"

Decorations

Cover the table with a white tablecloth. Use black streamers to form a border on the top edge of the table wide enough for the paper plates to lie on. Use white paper plates. When the table is set, it will give the appearance of the lights around a movie marquee or a makeup mirror. Make a sign which says "STARRING: (child's name)," put a picture of the birthday child under his or her name on the poster and stand it up in the middle of the table. You can also use toy cameras for decorations.

Hang pictures of popular actors, actresses and/or cartoon characters or ads for movies taken from newspapers on the walls. Black-and-white streamers can be draped from the ceiling to decorate the room.

Favors

Portrait of the Academy Award Winners

1 piece oak tag, any color
1 package small foil stars
    instant developing camera
    movie props

If you do not have an instant developing camera, borrow one to use on party day. Before party day, picture frames can be made by cutting a colored piece of oak tag so that, when a picture is glued to the middle, there will be a 3" border (frame) around it. Glue stars around the edge and also just outside the area where the picture will be. Fill a box with clothing and accessories that can be put on the children for the pictures. These props should relate to popular movies, if possible. Examples are a wide-brimmed hat like Scarlett O'Hara wore, moustache and hat like Rhett Butler's, Mickey Mouse ears, plastic glasses and fake nose, etc. One at a time, let the children pick out something to wear and pose for a picture, being sure to stand them in front of a good background. Take the picture from the waist up so that you have a nice, close shot. After the picture has developed, glue it onto one of the frames that was made.

Food

Movie Star Sandwich

1¼ grilled cheese sandwiches per person
  popcorn

Cut the grilled cheese sandwiches into four triangles each. You need five triangles for each sandwich. Lay out as shown in fig. 3 placing popcorn in the center.

fig. 3

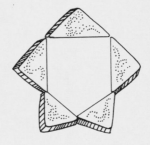

Shirley Temple

Serve ginger ale with a cherry in the glass to make it look like a cocktail.

Marquee Cake

1 package cake mix, any flavor
2 cans ready-made frosting (1 vanilla and 1 chocolate)
  vanilla wafers
1 tube cake decorating gel (brown)

Prepare mix according to package directions, using a 13″ x 9″ pan. Let cake cool. Measure a 2″ border all around the top of the cake and mark a line with a toothpick. Frost rectangle in the middle with white frosting. Frost outer border and sides of cake in brown frosting. Use vanilla wafers for lights on the marquee and write in the white rectangle as shown in fig. 4.

fig. 4

Games

Pass the Star

Make two stars from cardboard and cover them with aluminum foil.

Have the children form two lines, one behind the other. Give the first person in each line a star. Have the children pass the stars over their heads. When the person at the end of the line receives the star, he or she runs to the front of his line and starts passing the star back. The game ends when the person who was the first in one of the lines ends up being first again. Other versions of this game are passing the star under the legs or alternating over one's head and under the next one's legs.

Popcorn Race

For this game you will need an uncarpeted area with two lines of tape on the floor for the starting points and two lines of tape opposite these lines about 6 to 8 feet away for the finish line.

Have the children form two lines, one behind the other. Give each child a straw and a piece of popcorn. The first person in each line puts his or her piece of popcorn on the floor, gets on hands and knees, blows through the straw, pushing the piece of popcorn to the line on the other side of the room. He or she has to turn around and blow the popcorn back to the starting line. When the popcorn crosses the starting line, the next one on the team goes. The first team to finish wins the game.

Special Activity

Many local libraries have cartoons, movies and projectors that can be borrowed. There are also rental companies or camera shops that rent out movies and projectors, some at nominal fees and others at exorbitant fees, so check out all the possibilities before making your decision.

If you do not have a screen, you can use a plain white wall or hang a white sheet on a wall. Set up the chairs in rows like the movies or have the children sit on the floor in rows. If at all possible, have the movie area set up beforehand, preferably in a separate room to avoid moving everything around during the party.

CHAPTER IV

Pre- and Early-Teen Birthday Parties
(Ages 11-15)

Pre-teenagers and early teenagers try to act like adults and want to be treated as such. They can be encouraged to do most of the work for their own parties from beginning to end, and they can do it alone or with friends or relatives. Sit down with your child and discuss his or her ideas. Give suggestions, but try not to force your ideas on the child. Let the child feel he or she is making all the plans.

In this section, there are some plans in which the birthday child and his or her friends can make contributions to the preparations. In addition, we have included some parties where the birthday child can be responsible for all the preparations.

At the party, be sure to call attention to the work that the birthday child has done and thank any of the other children who helped in the preparation or the execution of the party to give them the feeling of pride and recognition they deserve.

Involve everyone in a game when they arrive. A good party starts the minute your guests arrive, so get them involved immediately! This serves as an "ice breaker," getting everyone acquainted.

THE BIRTHDAY BOWL

Tired of giving parties at home? In that case, have a segment of your party at a bowling alley. Teens enjoy bowling, and it's a bit of a change from holding the entire party in the house.

Invitations

What would you expect the invitation to a bowling party to look like? A bowling ball is one of the obvious answers.

1. Use 9" x 12" colored construction paper and fold in half lengthwise.

fig. 1

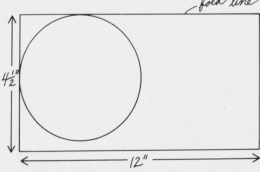

2. Use the lid from a ½-pound tub of margarine as a pattern for a circle with a 4″ diameter and draw it onto the folded construction paper with a small segment of the circle on the fold (see fig. 1).
3. Cut out the circle, leaving a bit of it attached at the fold line.
4. On the outer circle, cut three holes as finger holes in a bowling ball and use wording as in fig. 2.

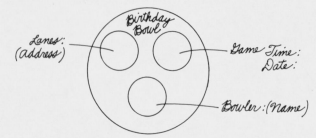

fig. 2

5. When you open the invitation, the words in the holes will appear inside, and you can write "RSVP BY: (date and phone number)" on the inside top.
6. NOTE: Be sure to ask the mothers for permission to take the teens bowling when the RSVP's are made.

Decorations

For an unusual decoration, make the table look like one of the lanes in a bowling alley. Put a brown tablecloth on the table and lay white or beige streamers down the length of the table with just a thin strip of the brown tablecloth showing between the steamers. From the ceiling above the table, hang bowling pins cut from white paper and a ball (balloon) from streamers. Draw holes on the balloon with a black felt-tip pen. Score cards made from oak tag can also be hung on the walls.

Favors

A popular favor for a bowling party is a small bowling set to take home for practice.

Marble Bowling
For each set:
10 round clothespins
1 marble
1 plastic sandwich bag
1 piece of ribbon

Use the clothespins (ten for each set) and the marble to make up a bowling set. The clothespins can be set up by standing them on their flat tops in rows as in bowling. They can be struck down with the marble. Put each set in a plastic bag and tie with a piece of ribbon.

Food

Balls and Pins

Serve meatballs and rotelle macaroni with tomato sauce.

"300" Delight

Serve root beer-flavored soft drink with a scoop of vanilla ice cream.

"Turkey" Cake

1 package yellow or white cake mix
1 can ready-made frosting (chocolate)

Prepare cake mix according to package directions, using a 2-quart casserole bowl or two 8" or 9" round pans. For the casserole, allow extra baking time and test cake as directed on package. Let cakes cool. If using round pans, frost as for a two-layer cake; for casserole, frost entire cake. To make it look like a bowling ball, cut three finger holes; using a small plastic pill container from the drug store, cut the three holes right through the frosting.

Games

Mix-Up Bowling

Make up a list of words relating to bowling and scramble up the letters of each word. Write the list of mixed up words down one side of a a sheet of paper, leaving the other half blank for the unscrambled words to be written in. Give each child a sheet of paper with the mixed up words. Let the guests unscramble the words as fast as they can. The first one to unscramble all the bowling words correctly is the winner.

The following are some suggested words that can be scrambled up:

strike (rtsiek)	lane (enla)	spare (rpaes)
gutter (truteg)	bowling (lnowgib)	ball (lbla)
turkey (rtykue)	pins (snpi)	split (tlpis)
score (rcsoe)	alley (ylael)	lockers (scrkeol)

Pass the Orange "Bowling Ball"

Form two lines, with everyone standing one behind the other. Give the first person on each team an orange and have him or her hold the orange under the chin and resting on the chest. The first person has to turn around and pass the orange from under his or her chin to the chin of the next one in line. The orange is passed in this manner until one team finishes passing. That team is the winner. If the orange falls during the passing, the team has to start over.

Special Activity

If there is a bowling alley in your area, take the party bowling. Serve lunch and the cake before leaving, and after bowling everyone can be taken home.

COOKING FUN

Young teens, whether they be boys or girls, greatly enjoy cooking. When planning this party, it is suggested that you invite a smaller group because the party will center around the kitchen and, as the old saying goes, "Too many cooks spoil the broth."

Invitations

Since this is a cooking party, the invitation should look like some type of food. An invitation shaped like a sandwich would be appropriate.

1. Using a piece of 9" x 12" white construction paper, fold in half widthwise and cut in half (see fig. 1).

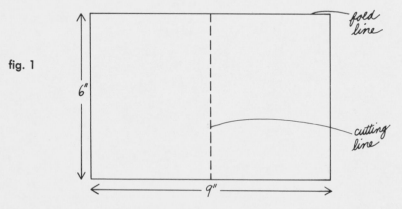

fig. 1

2. On front of the folded paper, trace a piece of bread with the top resting on the fold (see fig. 2).

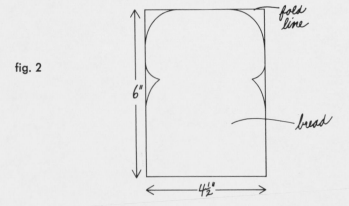

fig. 2

3. Around the edges of the front draw a thin line of brown with a crayon to give it the appearance of bread.

4. On the front, write:
   OPEN THIS BIRTHDAY SANDWICH TO SEE —
   HOW MUCH FUN THERE WILL BE —
5. Open up the invitation and, on the inside, write:
   MASTER CHEF: (name)
   KITCHEN LOCATION: (address)
   BAKING TIME: (time)
   LUNCH DATE: (day and date)
   RSVP BY: (date and telephone number)

Decorations

Your kitchen or a nearby room are practical areas for the party, and kitchen utensils and gadgets would be ideal for decorations. Some suggestions are: pots and pans (full or children's size), spoons, spatulas, menus, recipe cards with recipes on them and pictures of food. You can hang some of these decorations over the eating area.

Favors

Satisfy the teenage stomach, and the party will get rave reviews. Each of the cooks can return home with a scrumptious favor. Make up a brown paper lunch bag for each child. On the outside of each bag, write:
FAMOUS (guest's name)'s
CHOCOLATE-CHOCOLATE CHIP DROP COOKIES
The bag can be filled with cookies that are made as the Special Activity.

Food

Krazy Mixed-Up Sandwiches

Give each "cook" two slices of bread and some luncheon meat. Have each child choose a shape from some large cookie cutters and use it to cut the bread and meat, putting them together with mustard, ketchup, mayonnaise, etc. Put out a platter of olives, raisins, pimiento, cucumber slices, small carrot stick, small lettuce leaves, parsley and pickle slices so that each "cook" can decorate the sandwich as a funny animal, face or person. Everyone can vote on the funniest sandwich.

Chocolate Fizz

This drink can also be made by the partygoers. Fill a glass halfway with club soda. Add 2 tablespoons of chocolate syrup. Fill the rest of the glass with milk and stir well.

Sandwich Cake

1 package cake mix, any flavor
2 cans ready-made frosting (1 milk chocolate and 1 vanilla)
1 jar preserves, any flavor

Prepare cake mix according to package directions, using two 8" or 9" square pans. Let cakes cool. Cut both cakes as shown in fig. 3 to look like a slice of white bread.

fig. 3

Spread preserves on bottom layer and place top layer over it. Frost top of cake with vanilla frosting and then frost sides with milk chocolate. The cake will look like a jelly sandwich.

Games

Egg Roll

Form two equal teams and line up at one end of a room. Mark a line on the floor at the other end of the room with tape. Have the first person on each team get on hands and knees and push a hard-boiled egg in the shell to the line on the other side using his or her nose. When they reach the other side of the room, the players must turn around and push the egg back. When a player reaches the starting point, the next one in line goes. The first team to finish wins. Be sure that no other part of the body touches the egg other than the nose.

Toss the Beans in the Muffin Pan

Number each hole of a muffin tin with a score. Lay the pan on the floor. Give each person five beans. Have all the guests line up behind a marker and one at a time toss lima beans into the pan. See who can amass the highest score.

Special Activity

A good time to prepare the following cookies is after the sandwiches are eaten. Have everyone assemble in the kitchen.

Famous Chocolate-Chocolate Chip Drops

1 package chocolate cake mix
½ c. oil
2 eggs
1 c. (6 oz.) milk chocolate pieces
½ c. chopped walnuts

Preheat oven to 350° F. Blend cake mix, oil and eggs. Stir in chocolate pieces and walnuts. Using a teaspoon, drop onto an ungreased cookie sheet and bake 10 to 12 minutes. Have each child perform one step in the recipe so that everyone has a turn. They can also take turns dropping the cookies onto the cookie sheet. Be sure that while the cookies are baking, everyone is busy taking turns in the cleaning up. These cookies are then put in the bag described in the *Favors* section and, of course, everyone can have a taste at the party.

FIND THE TREASURE

From the pirates of the Seven Seas comes the theme for this party, which is sure to be a hit, since treasure hunts are intriguing and fun for all. The treasure can be any item, but few would be better than the birthday cake.

Invitations

Treasures can be found by fitting together clues. Make the invitation a map which has to be put together to be read.

1. Cut a piece of 9″ x 12″ construction paper in half to make two 9″ x 6″ rectangles.
2. On one rectangle, draw a freehand outline of your home state as large as possible. Cut on the lines.
3. The following is the wording for the invitation which can be written onto the cut out state:

TAKE A CAR, BOAT, TRAIN, PLANE OR WALK TO:
(address)
ON: (day and date)
AT: (time)
THERE YOU WILL FIND (name) WITH CLUES
FOR THE BIRTHDAY TREASURE HUNT
RSVP BY: (date and phone number)

4. After writing the information, cut the invitation into four or five random pieces and place the pieces in an envelope. Each guest will have to put the puzzle together to read the invitation.

Decorations

Hang a treasure map on the wall. This map can be of your hometown with arrows leading to your house or street. Cut out footprints from paper and hang these in a line, starting on a wall and going over the party table, into another room and then back to the same room again. On some of the footprints write things such as "hot," "hotter," "almost there," "cold," "colder," "freezing," etc. Hang colorful streamers over the party table. As a centerpiece for the table, you can make a large treasure chest out of any good-sized box. Cover the box with aluminum foil and fill the box with foil-covered chocolates, chocolate coins, hard candies and small treasures. Be sure the top of the box is covered.

Favors

A treasure box is an appropriate favor for a treasure hunt party. The box can be put to practical use at home. Here are the materials needed:
  heavy-duty aluminum foil
1 cigar box or similar container
6 pennies
  glue

Cover the cigar box with aluminum foil and glue in place. Glue the pennies to the top of the box.

Food

Silver Dollars

Use your favorite pancake recipe or a prepared mix to make small 2"-diameter pancakes. Since there is quite a bit of work involved in making the pancakes, they can be prepared just before the party and kept warm in an oven at a low-medium setting.

Berried Treasure Drink

Serve fruit punch with a strawberry in the bottom of each glass.

"Digging for Treasure" Cake

1 package cake mix, any flavor
1 can ready-made frosting (vanilla)
  brown sugar
1 measuring spoon (tablespoon)
  costume jewelry

Prepare cake mix according to package directions, using a 10" tube pan. Let cake cool. Frost entire cake with vanilla frosting, putting some extra frosting in the hole in the middle. Sprinkle brown sugar on top of the cake and on the sides, using a wide spatula to press the brown sugar onto the sides. Put the spoon end of the tablespoon in the hole and drape the costume jewelry around and into the hole.

Games

Gold Diggers Game

Using the table centerpiece and a large spoon, let each child take a turn scooping up a spoonful of treasures. Provide small plastic bags to put their treasures in. The one who scoops up the most in a single try is the winner.

Treasure Charades

A favorite game is charades. Apply a little creative thought to Treasure Charades and think of titles of books, songs, movies, sayings, etc., using coins or gems in their titles (*Examples: Diamonds Are a Girl's Best Friend,*

Pennies From Heaven, A Penny for Your Thoughts, Goldfinger, Silver Bells, The Pearl).

Make up slips of paper with one charade on each and put them in a treasure box (the birthday child's favor can be used). Have a child pick a paper without looking and act out what it says on the paper without talking. Everyone else has to try and guess what he or she is acting out. Everybody takes a turn in acting out a charade.

Special Activity

Find the Treasure

A treasure hunt requires some preparation before the party, but it is well worth the effort. You can hold it indoors so that the weather will not affect your plans. For a birthday treasure hunt, what better treasure can there be than the birthday cake. The guests all share in the solving of the clues and of course share in the eating of the cake. To prepare for a treasure hunt, make a list of about ten places to hide clues around the house. Make up a clue for each spot. Don't make it too easy or too difficult — just tricky.

Some suggestions for hiding places and clues are the following:

1. *Balloon hanging from ceiling or wall —*
   Bubble, bubble where are you,
   Inside me you'll find a clue.
2. *Refrigerator —*
   It's cold inside, but has to be
   To keep the clue heat-free.
3. *Under a sofa or chair cushion —*
   It's soft and comfy, as you know
   It will be found if you look low.
4. *On draperies —*
   I've been hung, not from a tree,
   On my outside, the clue will be.
5. *Under a rug —*
   Never sweep under me
   'Cause if you do, the clue won't be.
6. *Under a lamp table —*
   Over me, it is light,
   Look under me where it's like night.
7. *Book on a shelf —*
   I'm well-read and at the far right
   On fifty, the clue will be in your sight.
8. *Back of a door —*
   People always have to go through me,
   Look on my back where the clue will be.

9. *Fruit bowl —*
    A real nice place for a banana, apple or pear,
    Underneath, the clue will be there.
10. *Final clue leading to treasure —*
    Direct everyone to the location of the cake.

On a piece of paper, list each clue in the order in which the clues are being hidden. Save one as the starting clue to lead everyone to the first hiding spot. When they get to the first hiding spot, they must decipher the clue and go to the next spot, and so on. Be sure that the clue hidden in each spot is the one that leads them to the next spot. For instance, Clue #1 (the balloon) can be the starting clue which leads everyone to the balloon. In the balloon, they will find Clue #2 (refrigerator) and, after figuring out the clue, they will find the next clue in the refrigerator. The last clue should lead everyone to the treasure (the birthday cake). Hide the treasure in a place where you know nobody will look during the treasure hunt (try the shower). When the birthday cake is found, everyone can share in the rewards.

SOMETHING FROM NOTHING

All people get great satisfaction from creating something from nothing. Young teens are particularly interested in working with their hands, learning and creating. As the highlight and theme of a party, a craft activity is not only fun but is meaningful as well. As part of the "educational" value, the group should be involved in both the preparation and the "K.P."

Invitations

A novel idea for an invitation to a birthday party is one that resembles a help-wanted ad from the newspaper.

1. Using 9" x 12" white construction paper, fold in half lengthwise and then cut in half through the fold (see fig. 1).

fig. 1

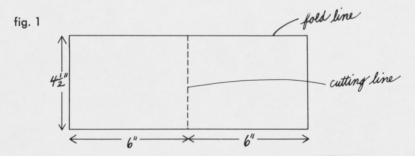

2. Using black felt-tip marker with a fine point, measure in ¼" around all four edges and make border lines on the outside page and on the right side of the inside.

3. On the outside, with the fold on the left, write:

> HELP WANTED
> Well-known birthday (girl, boy) is seeking assistance from an experienced maker of something from nothing. On second thought, experience is not necessary.

4. On the inside, write:

> YOU GOT THE JOB
> Report to Work
> On
> (date)
> At
> (address)
> Time
> See the Birthday (Girl, Boy)
> (name)
> RSVP BY:
> (date and phone number)

Decorations

Decorate the room with handmade crafts you or your child have made. If you can find pictures of bread dough crafts, hang them up on the walls. Drape streamers from the ceiling over the center of the table to the corners of the room. Hang kitchen utensils in a grouping over the center of the table.

Favors

As the Special Activity, the partygoers will be making the favors themselves.

Food

Be A Chef

Prepare a platter of meats, selecting the most popular cold cuts for the age group you invite. Place the meat platter along with a bread tray, platter of condiments, potato chips and/or salads on a table. Challenge all the partygoers to make something from nothing by creating their own luncheon delights.

Be A "Soda Jerk"

Put an assortment of soft drink flavors on the table along with a few flavors of ice cream, whipped cream, chopped nuts and cherries. Let everyone make his or her own float.

Rolling Pin Cake

1 jelly roll cake, already filled
    confectioners' sugar
2 round clothespins
    aluminum foil

Sprinkle jelly roll cake with confectioners' sugar. Cover clothespins with foil and insert one in either end of the cake with the round end sticking out of the cake.

Games

Placemat Game

In this game, form teams of two people each. With each team getting two placemats, everyone lines up at a starting line. Mark a line on the opposite side of the room (about 10 feet away). When told to "go," player #1 puts one placemat in front of player #2 (his or her partner), who steps on it with one foot. Player #2 then picks up his back foot and must balance on the other foot until player #1 picks up the back placemat and moves it in front of the one player #2 is stepping on. Play continues with player #1 moving one placemat in front of the other for player #2. The first pair to go to the opposite side of the room and back is the winning team.

Soft and Hard

Wrap up ten items used for cooking or baking in ten individual scarves or handkerchiefs and lay them out on a table. Form two teams. Have one team come to the table and let everyone on the team feel the wrapped items. This team then goes in another room with a pencil and paper. They must write down as many items as they can remember and identify. When they return, the other team does the same. After both teams are finished, the answers are checked and the team with the most right answers is the winner.

Special Activity

The following is the recipe for Bakery Fun Dough, which should be prepared within four hours of the time of the party. It can be prepared by the birthday child and will be used to make necklaces or plaques that can be taken home by your guests.

Bakery Fun Dough

4 c. flour
1 c. salt
1½ c. water

Combine all ingredients and mix well with hands until smooth. This recipe makes enough dough for 18 to 20 cookie shapes cut with medium-size cookie cutters. If you need more dough, make the recipe again. Do not double the ingredients. Divide the dough into individual plastic bags so it can be given out easily at the party.

REMEMBER: These cookies are ornaments and are NOT *edible*.

Set up a separate work table covered with newspapers and have a piece of waxed paper the size of a placemat at each place at the table for each child to work on. In the center of the table, place the following: two cookie sheets sprayed with nonstick cooking oil, spatula, water, an assortment of cookie cutters (preferably shapes requiring hairy features) and a garlic press. As the guests arrive, have them go to the table and start with Step #1.

1. Using a rolling pin, roll out the dough to ¼" thickness.
2. Cut out a cookie shape using a cookie cutter.
3. Using the spatula, lift the shape *carefully* and place on a cookie sheet.
4. If the shape requires hair or any hair-like features, put some of the excess dough in a garlic press and push it through. Use a knife to shear off the dough in the garlic press.
5. Using a finger, wet the area where the hair belongs. Lay the hair on the area.
6. Use a toothpick to make a hole in the top. Be sure that the cookie sheet can be seen through the hole.
7. Set oven at 350° F. and bake for 45 minutes until lightly browned. Take out and let cool on the cookie sheet.

While the dough is baking, you can continue with the party by serving the lunch and playing the games. When it is time to decorate the cookie shapes, lay out fluorescent paints in different colors, enough brushes for everyone and water. Let everyone paint his or her ornament. While the paint is drying, serve the birthday cake. After the paint is dry, spray with varnish on both sides and allow varnish to dry. The ornament can be nailed to a wall or hung by yarn or ribbon from a hook, door knob, or used as a necklace.

FARAWAY PLACES

From the far corners of the earth come ideas for stimulating and enjoyable parties. The rich customs and traditions of distant lands lend themselves to decorations, activities and food. Indeed, the United Nations flag could fly over your home for this birthday celebration.

Invitations

A picture postcard makes a most appropriate invitation to faraway places.

1. Use a 3" x 5" unlined index card and paste a picture of an airplane or anything related to a foreign country on one side (real picture postcards can be used instead of making the postcards).

2. Turn the card over and hold it with the 5" side on the top and bottom. Draw a vertical line down the center, dividing the card into two equal parts. On the right half of the card, write the name and address of the guest.
3. On the left half of the card in the upper right hand corner, write the date of the party and the time.
4. Then write:
   Dear (guest's name),

                     Wish you were here:
                        (address)
                  (Because it's my birthday,
                     hope you can come)
                          Fondly,
                  (Birthday child's name)
           P.S. RSVP BY: (date and phone number)
5. The invitation can be enclosed in an envelope or mailed as a postcard (the size is acceptable by the Post Office).

Decorations

Obtain travel posters, booklets or literature, if possible, from a local travel agency or airline. Hang the posters on the walls about the room. Make paper airplanes and hang them from the ceiling on streamers over the party table so they face in different directions. If you have any foreign dolls in their native costumes, these can be placed around the room either on walls, tables or hanging from streamers. Decorate the room with flags from around the world, if they are available. If not, the birthday child can make flags with colored construction paper.

Favors

European Checkers
   oak tag
   red construction paper
   2 pieces clear self-adhesive vinyl, 10" x 10"
   24 buttons — 12 each of two colors
   black felt-tip pen

Cut a 10" x 10" square piece of oak tag. Using black marking pen, draw a 1" border around the whole square. In pencil, rule 1" square boxes in the inner square. There will be eight squares across and eight squares down, making sixty-four squares. Make slits through the seven vertical lines, *leaving the border lines intact.* Cut red construction paper into eight 8" x 1" strips. Weave first strip of red paper, inserting through the slit on the oak tag from the bottom and continue weaving through rest of the slits. When weaving second strip, start by inserting strip into the slit from the top. Continue weaving all eight strips to form a checkerboard. Cover front and back with the self-adhesive vinyl. Use buttons for checkers and place in small plastic bag. Place the board and the bag of checkers into larger plastic bag.

Food

"French" Toast

Prepare French toast and serve it sprinkled with confectioners' sugar. You can purchase small foreign flags on toothpicks and stick one into each piece of French toast.

Tropical Drink

Serve fruit punch with an orange slice and a few strawberries in each glass. You can put a flag toothpick on the orange slice to make it look like a boat floating in the drink.

Little Italy Cake

1 package cake mix, any flavor
1 can ready-made frosting, any flavor
Prepare cake mix acording to package directions, using a 13" x 9" pan. Let cake cool. Cut out cake to resemble boot-shaped Italy (see fig. 4). Frost entire cake.

fig. 4

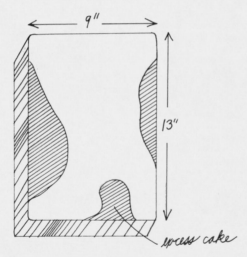

Games

Chinese Food

Form two teams and have the teams sit at a table opposite each other. Give the first player on each team two bowls — one containing some cooked rice (equal amounts for both teams) and one empty — and a set of chopsticks. Have the players use the chopsticks to transfer the rice from one bowl to the other. When the first player on each team has finished transferring the rice, he or she passes the two bowls and the chopsticks to the second player on the team, who then transfers the rice to the empty bowl. Each team continues in this manner until one team has finished and wins the game. This game can be loads of fun, particularly if the players are not familiar with chopsticks.

International Game

Give each guest a piece of lined paper and a pencil. Ask your guests to write the word "INTERNATIONAL" on top of their pieces of paper. Set a time limit during which the guests write down as many words as they can, using the letters in the word "international." The words have to be three letters or more. The one with the most correct words is the winner.

Special Activity

1. Ask all your guests to come to the party wearing one item of clothing suggesting a foreign country. Suggestions:

France — beret
Scotland — kilt
Mexico — sombrero and serape
Spain — cape and matador hat
Japan — kimono

The birthday child can prepare some popular songs from foreign countries to be sung at the party. It would be a nice touch if someone could play an instrument for the sing-along.

2. Take a trip to an airport or a boat dock if there is one in your area. If there is a cruise ship in port, inquire about going aboard. If you go to an airport, inquire about boarding a plane to see the inside.

WAY OUT GAMES

Here's a way to add a new flavor to the "thrill of victory and the agony of defeat." With Way Out Games, be as zany as you can. When conjuring up activities, remember the crazier the game, the more fun for the participants.

Invitations

Rubber tires are used for some crazy games. The invitation can be in the shape of a tire.

1. Use 9" x 12" black construction paper and fold in half lengthwise.
2. Use the lid from a ½-pound tub of margarine as a pattern for a 4"- diameter circle and draw it onto the folded construction paper with a small segment of the circle on the fold (see fig. 1).
3. Cut out the circle, leaving the segment attached at the fold line.
4. Cut a hole 1½" in diameter in the middle of the circle through both thicknesses.

5. With white crayon or ink, write the following on the outside:

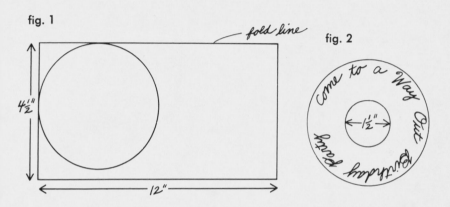

fig. 1

fold line

fig. 2

$4\frac{1}{2}''$

$12''$

$1\frac{1}{2}''$

come to a Way Out Birthday Party

6. Open up and write:

GAMES GALORE!
FIELD LOCATION: (address)
ACTIVITIES: (day and date)
(time)
COACH: (name)
RSVP: (date and phone number)

Decorations

Using a white paper tablecloth and colored tape, mark off the boxes for a hopscotch game (see fig. 3).

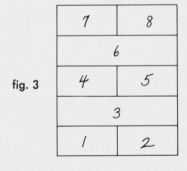

fig. 3

7	8
6	
4	5
3	
1	2

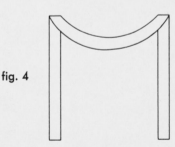

fig. 4

Write the numbers with a black felt-tip marking pen and lay the cloth on the table with the numbers facing the birthday child. Hang Frisbees, foam rubber blocks, small rubber or plastic foam balls and balloons on streamers from the ceiling. In a corner of the room, set up a prize booth with all the favors, candy and balloons. Decorate the corner by draping streamers as in fig. 4

Favors

Make up trophies for all your guests. Half of them will be for the winners and the rest wll be for the losers.

"Good Egg" Trophy

1 2½"-square flowerpot (plastic)
1 plastic egg from hosiery or any plastic egg that opens
    and will fit into the flowerpot
 india drawing ink
 glue
 fabric scraps

Glue fabric scraps onto the flowerpot to resemble patchwork. Glue the smaller half of the egg into the pot, leaving ¼" sticking out above the rim. Using a small scrap of paper, mix some of the ink with a bit of glue and draw a smiling face onto the top half of the egg, being sure it is right-side-up when put together with the other half. This is a winner's trophy. For the losers, draw a sad face (see fig. 5).

fig. 5

These trophies can be used to hold paper clips, coins, jewelry or any other small objects.

Food

The Un-Sandwich

Serve pizza for lunch, whether it be homemade, frozen or store-bought.

Moving Tire Drink

Using green (citrus) punch, make one big ice cube in a ring-shaped gelatin mold. Float the ice ring in a punch bowl filled with tropical fruit punch.

Obstacle Course Cake

1 package cake mix, any flavor
1 can ready-made frosting (vanilla)
 green food coloring
1 tube cake decorating gel (brown)
 red string licorice
2 Hershey's miniature chocolates

6 Chuckle Jelly Rings candies
7 Chuckle Spice Strings candies
5 Life Savers candies
  graham cracker crumbs or brown sugar

Prepare cake mix according to package directions, using a 13″ x 9″ pan. Let cake cool. Tint vanilla frosting green by dropping a few drops of food coloring into it and mixing. Frost cake with the green frosting and decorate as in fig. 6.

fig. 6

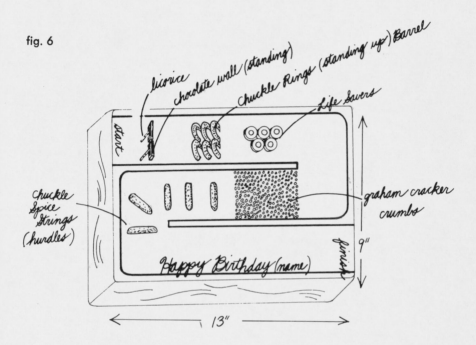

Games and Special Activity

Because there are quite a few Way Out Games to be played, the Games and Special Activity can be combined. As the guests arrive, they will be divided into two teams. Decide on a color for each team and cut up two pieces of colored construction paper, one color for each team. Put enough pieces of colored paper for everyone in a bag and, as the guests arrive, have each of them pick a piece of paper from the bag. When everyone has arrived, have them form two teams according to their colors. Make up a score sheet for each team with all the games listed and a space for the score on each. If a chalkboard is available, the scores can be written on it for all to see. All of the following games can be played in one room, one game at a time. Or if there is space, you can set up some of the games in another part of the house.

Bigfoot

Place a line of masking tape on the floor and tape a tape measure on the floor perpendicular to the line. Let everyone on one team take a turn placing one foot behind the line and trying to take the biggest step possible. Using the tape measure as a guide, the scorekeeper should mark down the length of each one's step and then add up the lengths for a team total. The team which steps the farthest wins the game.

Backwards Relay

Have the two teams form a line behind a starting line made with masking tape. At the opposite end of the room have two small wastepaper baskets. Give the first person on each team a clothespin. The contestant puts it between his or her knees and walks to the wastepaper basket without dropping it. As the contestants reach the baskets, they drop the clothespin in and walk backwards to tap the next one on the team. The first team to finish wins. If the clothespin falls before reaching the basket, the one who dropped it goes back to the starting line to start again.

Block Walk

Using six blocks, lay them out in a zigzag pattern 12" to 14" apart. Have one team form a line at the starting block and, one at a time, walk on the blocks to the end. Time them and add up each time for a team total. The team which does the Block Walk in the shortest time is the winner.

Hoopla

Have an unbiased person hold a Hula Hoop perpendicular to the floor and above it. Have one team at a time line up and take turns trying to get their bodies through the hoop without touching it. Each team member gets only one try, and the team that gets more people through the hoop without touching it is the winnner.

How Low Can You Go!

Have two people hold a broomstick about 12" from the floor. Have one team at a time line up and take turns trying to go under the stick without touching it. Each person gets only one try. The team which has more successes is the winner. If everyone can do it at 12" high, make the stick lower.

Small Obstacle Course

Set up two boxes (large enough to step into) next to each other, then a tire, then two more boxes. At the end, set a chair and a balloon to be blown up. Have one team at a time line up and take turns walking through the obstacle course, being sure one foot goes into each item on the floor. At the other end, each team member blows up a balloon, knots it and places it on the chair and sits on the balloon until it breaks. The team which does this in the shortest time is the winner.

CHAPTER V

Sweet Sixteen

Throughout the world, from the tribes in Samoa to the Great Plains in the United States, there has always been a ritual in some way relating to tribal custom or religion that heralds the coming of age of an individual. A young woman of today tells her group of peers that at Sweet Sixteen she has become a woman.

Long hair or short, bobby socks or bell bottoms; as each generation develops its own fads, customs and styles, one thing never changes — the sixteenth birthday is a milestone for a young lady. Some think of it as a coming out party, and to some it is as important as a debutante's ball. Songs have been sung, books have been written and movies made concerning this one important day in the life of a teenager.

A simple Sweet Sixteen party held at home can be as successful as the exotic outings many parents are known to have. With the proper attention and care, no matter what your budget, the birthday girl can have cherished memories to look back on for the rest of her life.

Where to Have a Sweet Sixteen Party

If you wish to hold a Sweet Sixteen party outside the home, there are many places the girls (and boys) can be taken. Among these places are restaurants, theaters, ice or roller skating rinks, or they can go horseback riding, on a boat ride or hayride or to a tennis club.

A Bit of Tradition

There are several traditions for a Sweet Sixteen party that would be pleasant to continue.

Sugar is the symbol of the sixteenth birthday, and a corsage made out of sugar, whether it be homemade or purchased, is usually given to the birthday girl.

At the party a hat is made for the birthday girl by sticking the bows from the gifts (as they are opened) on top of a gift box. Ribbon from the gifts can be used to hold the hat on the girl's head.

As the birthday girl opens the gifts, her comments should be written down on a napkin by one of her friends. When read back, it can be quite humorous out of context.

SLEEPY TIME

Teenage girls can talk all night when they get together for a slumber party. Be prepared to hear a lot of giggling and talking from their room late into the night, but warn them to keep it low after midnight.

Invitations

A bed and pillow make a nice invitation for a slumber party. Be sure to note on the invitations to bring sleeping bags, if the girls have them.
1. Use 9″ x 12″ pink construction paper and fold in half widthwise.
2. Cut this in half to make two smaller folded rectangles (see fig. 1).

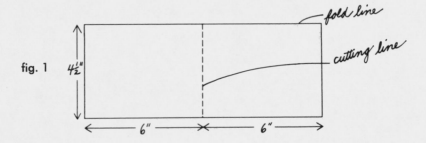

fig. 1

3. With the fold on the bottom, make a horizontal slit on the front piece 2″ from the top and 1″ in from either side.
4. Using white paper, cut a 2½″ x 5″ rectangle. This can be inserted in the slit on the pink paper (see fig. 2).

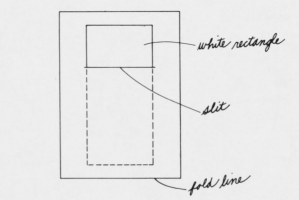

fig. 2

5. Glue the front and back pieces together around the three free edges.
6. Glue ½″-wide lace around three edges, omitting the top edge.

7. On the top of the white rectangle write:

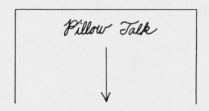

These two words should be visible when the white paper is pushed all the way into the slit.

8. Write the following on the white paper when you pull it out.

SAY! DID YOU HEAR . . . .
(name) IS HAVING A SWEET 16 SLUMBER PARTY
WHERE? (address)
WHEN? (day and date)
WHAT TIME: (time)
RSVP BY: (date and phone number)
DON'T FORGET P.J.'s, TOOTHBRUSHES AND
SLEEPING BAGS

Decorations

Because this is a slumber party and will take place in a bedroom, decorations are not necessary. There will be sleeping bags all over the room. If some girls do not have sleeping bags, use quilts or blankets folded in half. Be sure there is a source of music in the room, whether it be a radio or a record player.

Favors

Pet Pillow

1 terry cloth washcloth
1 piece of terry cloth cut to size of washcloth
   yarn (4-ply knitting worsted)
   needle & thread
   crochet hook
   scissors
   polyester filling

Using the two pieces of terry cloth, place right sides together and pin around edges. Sew around three and one-half sides, leaving a ¼" seam (half of the fourth side is left open for stuffing). Turn right side out and stuff. Sew the opening together on right side. Make fringes all around the pillow by cutting pieces of yarn 8" in length. Use eight strands of yarn for each fringe. Hold the group of eight strands and fold in half to form loops. Push crochet hook through double layer of terry cloth pillow ½" from edge. With hook pushed through the pillow, place the eight yarn loops on hook and pull yarn through the terry cloth, being sure all eight strands are pulled through. Pull yarn ends through the loop and pull on the ends firmly. Do this all around the edge of the pillow about ¾" apart.

Food

For a slumber party, the girls would come for dinner instead of lunch. Aside from preparing the dinner, have on hand plenty of snack food and drinks, because later on in the evening you can expect the girls to raid the refrigerator at least once.

Pigs in a Blanket

frankfurters
refrigerator crescent rolls
mustard
ketchup

Separate crescent roll dough into triangles. Spread each triangle with a mixture of mustard and ketchup. Wrap each frankfurter in a triangle, laying it on the wide end of the triangle and rolling up. Bake at 350° F. for 15 to 20 minutes, or until roll is golden brown. Serve with French fries and celery and carrot sticks on a bed of lettuce.

Sleeping Potion

Mix one part lemonade and one part grape juice.

"One Upon a Mattress" Cake

1 package cake mix, any flavor
2 cans ready-made frosting (1 vanilla and 1 chocolate)
2 Hostess Ho Ho's snack cake
1 piece cardboard, 9" wide and 7½" high
1 piece colored construction paper
flower cake decorations

Prepare cake mix according to package directions, using a 13" x 9" pan. Let cake cool. Lay cake with 9" edge on bottom and top. Using white frosting, frost top 4" of cake (to resemble a sheet). Frost remainder of cake with chocolate (blanket). Put flower cake decorations at random intervals on chocolate frosting. Round off two corners of the cardboard on one 9" side. Cover one side with colored paper. This is to be the headboard. Fold a 4" piece of aluminum foil over the straight bottom edge of the cardboard with 2" on either side. Place headboard on top end of cake and gently press onto the frosting. Lay the two Ho Ho's in front of the headboard, spacing evenly (pillows). Put shoes from an 11" doll next to the bed as props (see fig. 3).

Plan on serving breakfast the next morning. Some of the many breakfast foods that can be made are bacon, sausage, eggs, pancakes, hot or cold cereal and waffles. You will probably have enough time to feed

fig. 3

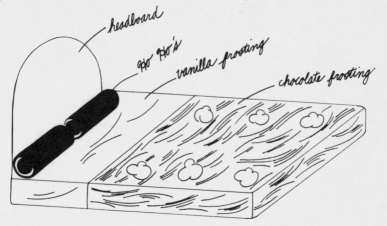

headboard

Ho Ho's

vanilla frosting

chocolate frosting

the rest of your family before the girls get up in the morning, since it is likely they will be up half the night. It might be a good idea to assign a bathroom coordinator for the morning.

Games

Pillow Talk

Have everyone sit in a circle on a pillow. The birthday girl is the leader and thinks of a sentence to whisper to the girl next to her, who, in turn, whispers to the next one. The sentence is passed around the circle. When it reaches the last girl, she announces what she heard, and the birthday girl announces the way the sentence started. It's amazing how the sentence has changed when it reaches the end!

Pajama Game

After all the girls are in their pajamas, have one girl lie on her back on the floor. The next one lies on her back perpendicular to the first with her head on the first girl's stomach. The next one lies down with her head on the second one's stomach. When everyone is lying down with her head on someone's stomach, the first girl can start by saying, "Ha." The next girl says, "Ha, Ha," the third says, "Ha, Ha, Ha," each one adding another "Ha." This game usually winds up as a roomful of laughing girls.

HAWAIIAN FEAST

America's truly magic isles in the Pacific provide an exotic surrounding for an important event. From the rich and beautiful Polynesian setting to the magnificent splendor of Diamond Head, the Hawaiian Islands have been a favorite since they were first discovered by Captain Cook in 1778.

Invitations

Palm trees are native to tropical climates. Therefore, a palm makes an appropriate motif for the invitation.

1. Using green 9" x 12" construction paper, fold in half widthwise, then cut in half through the fold as in fig. 1.

fig. 1

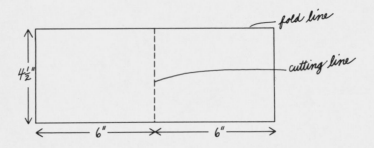

2. Holding the fold on top, cut out the shape of a palm tree with two leaves on either side as shown in fig. 2. Be sure to keep front and back attached at the fold on top of the leaves.

fig. 2

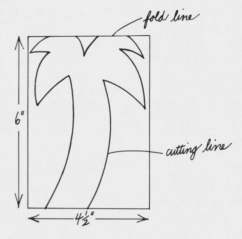

3. On the outside, write the following:
4. On the inside, draw three hearts one under the other. In the first one write "DATE," in the second write "TIME," and in the third write "PLACE." Be sure to write "RSVP" at the bottom.

Decorations

Try travel agents for posters with pictures of Hawaii and hang them around the room or, if you have made your plans well in advance, write to the Chamber of Commerce.

Using colorful tablecloths, set enough round tables in a room for everyone to sit at. Put a decorative candle in the middle of each table. If you have straw placemats, use them as place settings. Any tropical plants you have can be set around the room. Leis and straw hats are accepted symbols of Hawaii. They can be placed on the seats around the tables. Leis can be made from tissue flowers that have been strung together if you do not wish to purchase them.

Favors

Shell Necklace

Sixteen-year-old girls are most conscious of jewelry. Hawaii is known for its shells, which are made into necklaces. The necklaces can either be purchased, or you can create your own so that each girl can take one home as a favor.

Food

Banana Boat

Slice bananas in half lengthwise and cut each half into two pieces. Make a fruit salad with pineapple chunks, strawberries and blueberries. Place the fruit in a bowl with the banana slices around it. Sprinkle shredded coconut on top. When cutting up the pineapples for the fruit salad, remove fruit and core of the pineapple, leaving the shell which will be used for holding the drinks. Be sure that the shell stands upright. If it doesn't, adjust by slicing a piece from the bottom.

Sweet and Sour Spareribs

1 9-oz. jar mustard
1 10-oz. jar grape jelly
1 1-lb. 4-oz. can pineapple chunks
3 lbs. spareribs

Combine mustard and jelly in a pot and heat to a boil. Marinate ribs in sauce for 1 hour. Remove ribs from marinade and put in a shallow pan. Save sauce. Bake ribs at 450° F. for ½ hour. Pour off excess fat. Turn oven to 350°, add pineapple to sauce and pour over ribs. Bake for 1 hour or until ribs are tender when pierced with a fork. Cut spareribs into individual pieces with kitchen shears or a sharp knife. Serve over white rice. If desired, more sauce can be made to pour over the white rice.

(makes 3 to 4 servings)

Luau Platter

Prepare a platter of kumquats, cherry tomatoes, cucumber slices and carrot sticks. Lay out on a bed of lettuce.

Polynesian Punch

Combine equal parts of pineapple juice and ginger ale to make an interesting drink. Put juice into a small soft drink bottle (about 16 oz.). Put crushed ice into the pineapple shell saved from the fruit salad and put the bottle into the shell. The size of pineapples varies, so you might have to omit the ice and use the shell as a decoration for the bottle.

Pineapple Cake

1 package cake mix, any flavor
1 can ready-made frosting (chocolate)
1 tube cake decorating gel (yellow)
    leafy top of a pineapple

Prepare cake mix according to package directions, using a 13" x 9" pan. Let cake cool. Cut cake as shown in fig. 3.

fig. 3

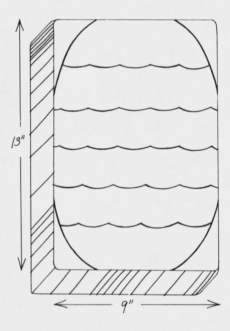

Frost the cake. Using decorating gel, make scallops on cake to resemble a pineapple. Take the top of the pineapple and cut off where leaves meet fruit. Slice in half lengthwise so it will lie flat. Place at the top of the cake.

Games

Hawaiian Memory

Gather as many items as you can relating to Hawaii and place them on a tray. Give a pencil and a piece of paper to each guest. Bring the tray into the party room and have everyone study it for one minute. Take the tray out of the room and have everyone write down as many items as they can remember. The one who has the most correct answers is the winner.

Banana Game

Have two girls sit opposite each other. Blindfold them and give each one a peeled banana. Have them try to feed each other the bananas. After the first two are finished, another two girls try their luck. This can turn out to be a hilarious proceeding. It might also be slightly messy.

Special Activity

Play some Hawaiian music, have everyone stand in line and let the birthday girl teach all the girls the hula. The birthday girl, in most cases, will have to do some research and learn how to do it beforehand. For this activity, the birthday girl can wear a grass skirt.

CHAPTER VI

Eighteen Years Old:
The Coming of Age

We can all think back to those teenage years when we were perhaps sixteen or seventeen; yet, when asked our age, we seemed to push it ahead to eighteen. Today, of course, no matter what our age, we like to push it back a few years. Witness the late Jack Benny, who never quite passed his 39th birthday.

Eighteen was important in the good old days and is still important to the young person obtaining a driver's license, entering the job market or going on to college. Indeed, eighteen is a milestone birthday, marking the when a "kid" becomes a "person."

Since 1968, eighteen brings with it the right to vote and the full burden of being responsible for oneself and no longer being a "minor." It is an important occasion, not only for the individual but for the entire family.

CABARET

If "Life is a cabaret . . . ," then it is at eighteen that the cabaret comes to life. The excitement, the music, the food and the flavor of the cabaret can be brought into your home to commemorate a birthday and symbolize the new experiences in life that await the birthday celebrant.

Invitations

Since a cabaret usually has music, whether it be live or recorded, the invitation can be shaped like a record.

1. Using 9" x 12" black construction paper, fold in half lengthwise.
2. Use the lid from a ½-pound tub of margarine as a pattern for a 4"-diameter circle and draw it onto the folded construction paper with a small segment of the circle on the fold (see fig. 1).
3. Cut out the circle, leaving the small segment attached at the fold line.
4. From yellow construction paper, cut out a small circle 2" in diameter.
5. Glue the yellow circle to the black circle on the outside of the invitation, centering the yellow circle. Make a small black circle in the center of the yellow circle for the hole in the record.

6. On the outside, in the yellow circle, write: RECORDED BY (name).
7. On the inside, with white ink or white crayon write wording as in fig. 2.

fig. 1

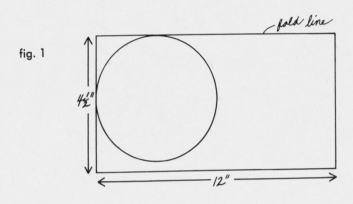

fig. 2

Decorations

Set up card tables and chairs around a fairly large room. Leave a space in the middle for dancing. Set the tables with white linen tablecloths and napkins to give a formal atmosphere to the room. Place a vase on each table with fresh or artificial flowers. Make up a folded card to stand on each table. Write "Reserved" on it and the names of the four people who are to sit at the table. In one corner of the room, or in a separate room, set up a long table for hors d'oeuvres and dessert. Lay out dinnerware on the table (not paper).

Music is needed for this party. Have either a band or records for dancing. Dimming the lights will add atmosphere. Drape streamers at the entranceway to the room and hang a cluster of balloons over each table.

Buffet de Cabaret

Little Records

8 oz. shredded cheddar cheese
3 onions, diced

mayonnaise
cocktail rye bread

Mix cheese, onions and mayonnaise together. Use enough mayonnaise to make a paste. Spread on cocktail rye. Bake at 350° F. for 5 minutes or until golden brown.

(makes 2½ to 3 dozen hors d'oeuvres)

Turkey Fingers

1 white meat turkey roast, cooked & cooled
  ketchup
  mayonnaise
  slivered almonds

Cut turkey into ½" slices and then into triangles. Mix mayonnaise and ketchup together to make Russian dressing. Put a toothpick in each piece of turkey and dip into dressing and then into almonds. This looks especially nice served on a bed of lettuce.

(makes 35 to 40 hors d'oeuvres)

Cranberry-Chili Franks

2 lbs. cocktail frankfurters
1 large can jellied cranberry sauce
1 jar chili sauce

Combine chili sauce and cranberry sauce in a pot and heat until cranberry sauce dissolves. Cook frankfurters and add to sauce. Serve hot with toothpicks.

Cabaret Log

2 8-oz. pkgs. cream cheese
1 8-oz. can crushed pineapple
2 tbsp. minced onion

¼ c. chopped green pepper
2 c. finely chopped walnuts
1 tbsp. seasoned salt

Soften cream cheese. Add pineapple, 1 cup nuts and other ingredients. Mix with hands and refrigerate 1 hour. Shape into a log and put the rest of the nuts on waxed paper. Roll the log in nuts. You can decorate the log with maraschino cherries and/or a pineapple ring. Serve on a platter with crackers.

(makes 48 to 60 servings)

Happy Time Punch

2 cans Hawaiian Punch (Very Berry or Cherry Royale) fruit beverage
2 bananas, sliced

2 oranges, sliced
1 pint fresh or frozen strawberries
  vodka (optional)
Mix all ingredients and chill. Serve in a punch bowl.

(makes 28 4-oz. servings)

Dessert
Disco Cake

1 package cake mix, any flavor
2 cans ready-made frosting (1 vanilla & 1 chocolate)
  black gumdrop
Prepare cake mix according to package directions, using two 8" or 9" round pans. Frost bottom layer on sides and top with chocolate. Lay the second layer on top. Using a lid from a ½-pound margarine tub (or any other circle with 4" diameter), gently press down into center of top of cake to mark a circle. Frost center circle with white up to the mark. Frost around the rest of the top with chocolate and around the sides. Using the tines of a fork, make grooves in the chocolate frosting on top of the cake. Place a black gumdrop in the center to look like the hole in the record. On white "label" write "Happy Birthday." Serve with coffee and/or tea.

Games

Multiplication Dance

This is an old favorite that can be used as an "ice breaker." With the music playing, have the birthday person pick a partner to dance with (it is usually a slow dance). After one minute of dancing, stop the music, have the couple split up and have each person pick a new partner. There are now two couples dancing. Again, after a minute of dancing, have the music stop and let the couples split up and take new partners. Continue doing this until everyone in the room is dancing, including the wallflowers.

Dancing Statues

Everyone should be dancing (preferably a fast dance) for this game. One person is "it" and does not dance. Each time the music stops, all the dancers must freeze. If either partner of a couple is caught moving when the music stops, that couple leaves the dance floor. Everyone must stay "frozen" until "it" says "relax." The music starts again and dancing continues until it is stopped and everyone has to freeze again. This continues until there is one couple left on the floor.

Special Activity

Ask someone you know who sings, acts or dances to entertain at the party. Another suggestion is to have a talent show. Ask your guests beforehand to prepare little acts to perform at your party.

BEACH BALL

You need not live on the Riviera, the shores of Cape Cod or on the southern coast of California to throw a beach party. By substituting a little imagination for the sand and the surf, your own private beach can be created in your home. Of course, if a beach is convenient to you, be it a river, lake or ocean, your birthday gala can be that much more exciting and realistic.

Invitations

A life preserver is a necessity at the beach. Your invitation can resemble one.

1. Using 9" x 12" white construction paper, fold in half lengthwise.
2. Use the lid from a ½-pound tub of margarine as a pattern for a 4"-diameter circle and draw it onto the folded construction paper with a small segment of the circle on the fold (see fig. 1).

fig. 1   fig. 2

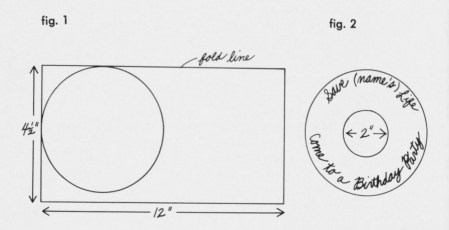

3. Cut out the circle leaving the small segment attached at the fold line.
4. Cut a hole 1½" in diameter in the middle of the circle through both thicknesses as in fig. 2 and write the following.
5. On inside write:

ADDRESS:

TIME: DATE:

RSVP BY: (date and phone number)

Decorations

If you are having the party indoors, decorate the room to look like a beach. Hang fishermen's net from the ceiling with toy boats and artificial fish. Place beach balls all around the room. If possible, get pictures of people in different styles of bathing suits, from "way back when" to the present. Make waves from blue construction paper and put the pictures above the waves on a wall.

Set up card tables and chairs around the room. Use earth tones for tablecloths and other paper goods. Large shells can be placed on the tables for decorations. Pails and shovels can be used as centerpieces, with a plant in each pail. The plants can be used as prizes.

Food

Barrel Lunch

Make up one barrel (large plastic container) for each couple. If the young men and women do not come to the party as couples, you can pair them off. In each barrel put four pieces of chicken, two servings of potato salad, two servings of cole slaw and two dinner rolls. Have "second helpings" available on a table. If you have favorite recipes for potato salad and cole slaw, use them. Otherwise, most supermarkets and delicatessens have potato salad and cole slaw which is usually quite good.

Favorite Fried Chicken

eggs
seasoned bread crumbs
chicken pieces (allow at least two pieces per person)
cooking oil

Mix eggs in bowl. Put bread crumbs in another bowl. Heat oil in pan on medium heat until hot. Dip pieces of chicken in egg and then into bread crumbs, being sure to cover completely. Put chicken in hot oil and cook on one side until it is golden brown and then turn over to cook other side. When brown on both sides, remove from pan and drain on absorbent paper. Let chicken cool.

Sunshine Smash

Mix equal parts of iced tea and lemonade to make a refreshing drink.

Fish Cake

1 package cake mix, any flavor
1 can ready-made frosting (vanilla)
red food coloring
yellow food coloring
maraschino cherry

Prepare cake mix according to package directions, using a 13" x 9" pan. Let cake cool. Cut and arrange as illustrated in fig. 3.

fig. 3

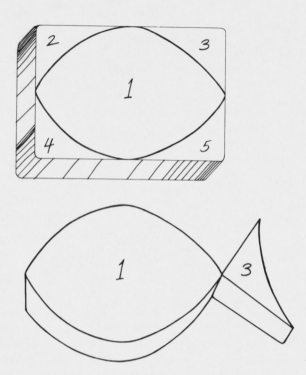

Tint the vanilla frosting orange by mixing red and yellow food coloring into it. Use a small amount of frosting to stick the tail of the fish to the body. Frost the entire cake and use a maraschino cherry for an eye.

Games

Life Savers ®Game

Form two teams and have them line up at one end of the room. Fill two cups with Life Savers ®(allow two Life Savers per person and split them up evenly between the two cups). Place one cup on either side of a card table which is at the opposite side of the room. Put two chairs next to the table, one on either side. Next to each seat have a blindfold and a piece of yarn 2 feet long with a Life Saver tied to one end. Have one person from each team act as a blindfolder and stand behind the chair on his side. When everyone is ready, have the first person on each team go across the room as fast as possible, sit in the chair and be blindfolded by their teammates who then hand them the pieces of yarn and give each one a Life Saver from the cups. The blindfolded person must string two Life Savers, put the yarn down on the table, take off the blindfold and go across the room to tap the next one on his or her team. The team who finishes first is the winner.

Don't Get Wet

Use a large, wide tub or pot and fill it with water. Be sure the floor under it is covered. Float a few apples in it. One at a time, let each guest try to grab an apple with his or her mouth and lift it out of the tub. Remember, no hands allowed!

Special Activity

As a Special Activity, the party can be held at a beach. The food is portable and playthings such as Frisbees, a volleyball and net and beach balls can be taken along.

ZODIAC PARTY

First, mix one Libra with one Virgo: add one Pisces and season with a Gemini plus assorted other signs. Second, check your rising suns, planets, houses and moons; then proceed full speed ahead for a captivating and spellbinding Zodiac Party.

Invitations

An invitation that is worded like a horoscope will give all the guests an idea of what the party will be like. It is a simple but unusual invitation.

1. Fold a sheet of 9″ x 12″ white construction paper in half lengthwise.
2. Cut the folded paper in half to form two folded rectangles as in fig. 1.

fig. 1

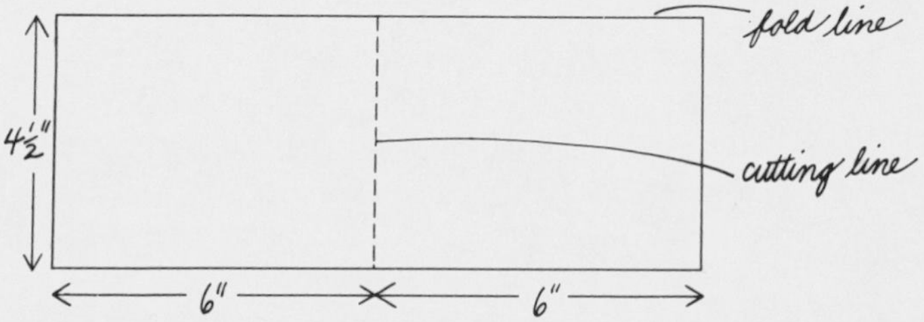

3. With the fold on left, write: YOUR HOROSCOPE FOR (date of party) IS:
4. On the inside of the invitation, write: "You are a warm, witty and intelligent person. You will be at (name)'s house at (address) at (time). You will have a good time with other people who will all be gathered at the above place for the same reason — a Birthday Party!"

Decorations

Since the zodiac is related to the planets, the party room can be decorated with the planets, the sun and the moon. Blow up balloons for all the planets — Mercury, Venus, Earth, Mars, Jupiter, Saturn, Uranus, Neptune and Pluto — and write the name of each planet on a balloon with a felt-tip marking pen. Hang them from the ceiling on streamers. Cut out stars from cardboard and cover with aluminum foil. Hang the stars from streamer as was done for the balloons. The tablecloth, paper plates, paper cups and napkins can be the color of the birthday person's birthstone.

Another nice touch is to find out the birth dates of everyone attending the party and prepare a little scroll for each that relates to his or her zodiac sign. Roll up the paper and tie with a narrow ribbon. Make up a name card for each guest, punch a hole in it, attach to the ribbon and use as a place card. The following is a bit of astrological information that can be used for the scrolls.

(Ram); March 21-April 20; Planet ruling Aries — Mars; represents new life; Aries people are leaders, idealists; keywords — cooperation, passion, ardor; birth gems — opal and bloodstone; color — red.

(Bull); April 21-May 20; planet ruling Taurus — Mars; represents strength, power; Taurians like the good things in life; keywords — endurance, stamina; birth gems — amethyst, diamond; color — red-orange.

(Twins); May 21-June 21; planet ruling Gemini — Mercury; represents discussion or exchange of opinion; Gemini people are stimulating and charming; keywords — intellect, diversity; birth gems — emerald, lapis lazuli; color — orange.

(Crab); June 22-July 22; planet ruling Cancer — moon; represents tenacity; Cancer people are home-loving; keywords — expansion, tenacity; birth gems — aquamarine, sapphire; color — orange yellow.

(Lion); July 23-August 22; planet ruling Leo — sun; represents rulership; Leo people are loyal, generous; keywords — courage, assurance; birth gems — ruby, emerald, black onyx; color — yellow.

Virgo

(Virgin); August 23-September 22; planet ruling Virgo — Mercury; represents honesty, purity; Virgo people are more intellectual than emotional; keywords — chastity, purity; birth gems — diamond, jasper, sardonyx; color — yellow-green.

Libra

(The Balance); September 23-October 22; planet ruling Libra — Venus; represents friendliness, cooperation, justice; Libra people are sociable and gay; keywords — justice, equilibrium; birth gems — pink jasper and opal; color — green.

Scorpio

(Scorpion); October 23-November 21; planet ruling Scorpio — Mars, Pluto; represents strength; Scorpio people have a passion for hard work; keywords — originality, desire; birth gems — topaz, beryl; color — green-blue.

Sagittarius

(The Archer); November 22-December 20; planet ruling Sagittarius — Jupiter; represents directness and the spreading of knowledge; Sagittarians are open and honest; keywords — insight, reason; birth gems — turquoise, moonstone; color — blue.

Capricorn

(Goat); December 21-January 19; planet ruling Capricorn — Saturn; represents indifference; Capricorn people are ambitious; keywords — discrimination, understanding; birth gems — white onyx, garnet, ruby; color — deep blue.

Aquarius

(Man Pouring Water); January 20-February 18; planet ruling Aquarius — Saturn, Uranus; represents servant of man; Aquarians give of themselves; keywords — loyalty, fellowship; birth gems — sapphire, jade, ruby; color — indigo.

Pisces

(Fish); February 19-March 20; planet ruling Pisces — Jupiter, Neptune, Pluto; represents agreeable companionship; Pisces people have a love for beauty; keywords — appreciation, peace, sympathy; birth gems — pearl, opal, moonstone; color — violet.

Food

Hors d'Oeuvres

Planetary Platter

egg salad
tuna salad
deviled ham
1 loaf day-old white bread

Using cookie or canapé cutters shaped like stars, crescent moons and circles, cut out white bread. Put egg salad, tuna salad or deviled ham on each bread shape, using a pastry bag, knife or spoon. Use a stuffed green olive slice as a topping. Lay out all the shapes on a platter.

"Cancer the Crab" Dip

1 8-oz. package cream cheese, softened
½ c. mayonnaise
1 tsp. Worcestershire sauce
1 tbsp. grated onion
6 oz. can crab meat
2 tsp. lemon juice
3 tbsp. chili sauce

Mix all the ingredients together and chill for 8 to 10 hours. Serve dip with sesame bread sticks and assorted crackers.

Saturn Snacks

1 can whole water chestnuts
3 tbsp. soy sauce
1 tbsp. sugar
bacon slices, cut in half crosswise

Mix soy sauce and sugar and marinate water chestnuts in this mixture for about 1 hour. Drain off marinade and wrap each water chestnut in a piece of bacon. Secure with a toothpick and place on a broiler pan or on a rack in a shallow pan. Bake at 350° F. for about 25 minutes or until the bacon is crisp.

(makes 20 hors d'oeuvres)

Potato Moons

3 cups cooked instant mashed potatoes
2 packages refrigerator crescent rolls
instant minced onion (optional)

Add minced onion to potato mixture, if desired. Unroll crescent roll dough and cut each triangle into two smaller triangles. Using a rolling pin, roll out each triangle until almost double in size. Put a tablespoon of potato in the center of a triangle. Bring two points of the triangle together over the potato mixture and press together. Bring the third point over and around to seal in the potato. Pinch together all open spaces. Bake at 375° F. on an ungreased cookie sheet for 15 to 20 minutes or until golden brown.

(makes 32 hors d'oeuvres)

Punch
House of the Rising Sun Punch

16 oz. orange juice
16 oz. pineapple juice
16 oz. lime juice
64 oz. ginger ale
 1 quart orange sherbet

In a punch bowl, mix fruit juices and add sherbet. Put ice in the bowl. Add ginger ale just before serving.

(makes 28 4-oz. servings)

Dessert
Zodiac Cake

1 package cake mix, any flavor
1 can ready-made frosting (vanilla)
1 tube cake decorating gel (brown)
  colored construction paper
  toothpicks

Prepare cake mix according to package directions, using two 8" or 9" round pans. Let cakes cool. Frost with white frosting to make a two-layer cake. Using colored paper, cut out twelve strips of paper 1" x 3". Fold each one in half and glue around a toothpick with the toothpick on the fold. On each little flag write one sign or symbol of the zodiac. On the center of the cake, use cake decorating gel to write the zodiac symbol of the birthday person. Place the flags around the cake as in fig. 2.

fig. 2

Games

Star Gazer Game

One person is the Star Gazer who, beforehand, arranges to have another person work with him or her. The other person tells the Star Gazer the word he will write on a piece of paper during the game.

To start the game, the Star Gazer hands out small slips of paper and pencils to everyone in the room (don't forget, the "cohort" is among them), telling them to write down a word on their papers and fold them up. The

Star Gazer collects the papers, putting the "cohort's" paper at the bottom of the pile. The Star Gazer sits on a chair in the middle of the room and puts the first paper to his forehead and closes his eyes as if to concentrate on trying to see what is written on the paper. He then announces the word he previously arranged with the "cohort" who, in turn, says "That's mine, you're right!" The Star Gazer then opens the paper as if to check it when he actually is looking at the next word he will be guessing (the "cohort's" paper was on the bottom of the pile). He then holds the next paper to his forehead and says the word he just saw on the paper. Play continues with the Star Gazer seeing the next word before he holds a paper to his head. Everyone will be amazed and mystified by this trick.

Star Game

This is played like the old game of "Buzz." Everyone sits in a circle. The first person starts by saying "one," the next one says "two," and so on. The people keep counting until they get to "nine." The one who is supposed to say "nine" says "star" instead; the next one says "ten." When they get to "eighteen," instead of saying the number, that person says "star." The counting continues around the group with the players saying "star" instead of "nine" a multiple of "nine" or any numbers containing a "nine" such as "19." If a player says the number instead of "star," that player is out. Or if a player says "star" when it is not called for, the player is out.

Special Activity

1. Everyone can read the zodiac information written on the scroll found at his or her place at the table. It is interesting to hear about other people's astrological signs.
2. Eighteen-year-olds enjoy talking and dancing. For this party, music is a necessity. Even if none of the guests want to dance, they still like listening to the music while they talk.

CHAPTER VII

Thirty Years Old

Both authors of this book can tell you of the countless hours of sleep lost and the fear and trepidation they felt when approaching that horrible thirtieth birthday — "my lord, that is old." As we looked at ourselves, respectively mothers of two children, married for about a decade and well entrenched in our families and our homes, the thought of being thirty was almost impossible to accept.

When you consider the life expectancy of people today, thirty is one fantastic birthday to celebrate. If ever one is in the "prime" of his life, that prime most definitely begins at thirty. If every decade of your life were an inning in a baseball game and you expected to live to be ninety, it is only the third inning and you don't even have a complete game until after the fourth inning.

The thirties are an ideal time to enjoy life. While still having youth in your bones, you have age in your mind and can live each day or year to the fullest. Take advantage of the thirties and commemorate each year. A birthday party will not only celebrate, but will become a social opportunity to share a meaningful day with close friends. It could even be considered a good reason to have a simple cocktail party. Planned and created with your guests in mind, it can be a blast.

SCAVENGER HUNT—SURPRISE PARTY

A surprise party can be as exciting and rewarding for the person giving it as for the people attending it. A little thought must be given to the planning of the party; specifically, when to set up for the party, where to keep everything and how to keep the guest of honor away from the party site while everything is being readied.

The first and most important thing is to remember to write on the invitation that the party is a surprise and to indicate a *prompt* time of arrival. You wouldn't want anyone to "let the cat out of the bag." Also, indicate a time to RSVP when you know the guest of honor will be out of the house. It could be awkward to have him or her answer the phone when someone calls to RSVP.

The ideal situation for a surprise party is to hold the party at a friend's or relative's house. In this case, there would be no problem keeping everything under wraps. You could make arrangements to buy all the necessary food and decorations for the party and set everything up beforehand. Another easy surprise party is one held in a restaurant. Everyone meets at the restaurant and the guest of honor is taken there.

If the party is being held in the home of the guest of honor, it will not be as easy to keep it a surprise. Make arrangements with a neighbor or friend to keep all the food and any other things for the party.

Keeping the guest of honor away from the scene of the party can be quite difficult. As a matter of fact, this is the hardest part of a surprise party. First, consider the guest of honor's daily routine. You don't want to deviate from the routine too much and cause suspicion. Also, decide how much time will be needed to decorate, lay out the food and have all the guests arrive. When you have given thought to the aforementioned, decide on a way to keep the guest of honor out of the house. Try to have someone who knows about the surprise keep the guest of honor occupied. Here are several suggestions:

Have a friend take the guest of honor to play golf, go bowling, play tennis, go to a movie or just go on an errand.

If you have a babysitter, you can go out to visit friends that are invited to the surprise party and, after a while, have the babysitter call the friends' house and say that the electricity is not working and there are no lights on. You will have to return home to check the situation.

Take the guest of honor out for dinner in a restaurant and then return to the scene of the party.

The guest of honor can be involved in his own surprise party without being aware of it, as in the Scavenger Hunt which is explained later.

Invitations

When making or purchasing invitations for this party, the invitation should inform the guests that the party is a surprise and should give a good time to call. It should also give a *prompt* time of arrival.

1. Using 9" x 12" colored construction paper, fold in half lengthwise and then cut in half through the fold as in fig. 1.

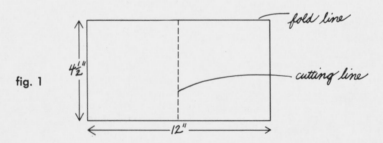

fig. 1

2. With the fold on top, write the following on the outside:

A BALL
A DOLL
A BOX
A CHAIR
A GRANDPARENT

3. On the inside, write: CAN YOU FIND THESE THINGS? IF SO, THEN YOU QUALIFY FOR A SCAVENGER HUNT-*SURPRISE PARTY* FOR (name).

> AT: (address)
> DATE: (day and date)
> TIME: (*prompt* time)
> RSVP BY: (date, phone number and good time to call)

Decorations

There are no decorations necessary for this party, since the people on the Scavenger Hunt will bring the decorations with them. The only thing necessary is a long table set up for the hors d'oeuvres and dessert.

Food

Hors d'Oeuvres

Onion-Stuffed Pineapple

1 pineapple
1 pint sour cream

1 envelope onion soup mix
⅓ cup finely chopped walnuts

Mix onion soup, sour cream and nuts together to make a dip. Cut off the top of a pineapple and scoop out the fruit. Save the fruit for the dessert recipe. If the pineapple shell doesn't stand upright, slice a piece off the bottom so it stands flat. Put onion dip into the pineapple shell. If the shell is large and the dip doesn't fill the shell, cut it down on the sides a bit. Put pineapple shell in the center of a round platter with potato chips, corn chips or crackers around it for dipping.

Cheese Logs

1 8-oz. pkg. cream cheese
1 3-oz. pkg. cream cheese
2 egg yolks
½ c. sugar

½ lb. sweet butter
1 tbsp. cinnamon
½ c. sugar
2 loaves thin-sliced white bread

Remove crust from bread and roll thin. Mix cream cheese, egg yolks, ½ c. sugar. Using a spatula or knife, spread thin to cover each bread slice. Roll up each slice like a jelly roll. Cut roll in half. Melt butter. Mix the other ½ c. sugar and cinnamon together. Dip each roll into butter to cover and then into the sugar and cinnamon mixture. (Refrigerate or freeze, if desired, after preparing recipe to this point.) To serve, return to room temperature. Place on an ungreased cookie sheet and bake at 350° F. for 20 to 25 minutes.

(makes 55 hors d'oeuvres)

Surprise Puffs

1 c. boiling water
½ c. salted butter

1 c. flour
4 eggs

Combine boiling water and butter until butter melts. Add flour all at once. Reduce heat. Cook until one big ball is formed and it leaves the sides of the pot. Remove from heat. Cool for a few minutes. Stir in eggs one at a time. Drop batter by teaspoon onto ungreased cookie sheet. Bake at 350° F. for 30 minutes. Puncture with a toothpick to release steam. Cool. Cut tops off and fill.

Filling:

3 c. cooked chicken, minced
½ c. chopped celery
¾ c. mayonnaise

¼ c. chopped almonds
¼ c. raisins

Mix all ingredients together. Put chicken salad into cream puffs with a teaspoon and replace tops. These look nice served in miniature cupcake papers.

(makes 50 puffs)

Oriental Balls

3 lbs. ground beef
½ c. soy sauce
1 tsp. instant minced onion

½ tsp. ground ginger
½ c. water

Combine all ingredients in a large bowl. Form meat into 1" balls and place uncovered in a shallow baking pan. Bake at 350° F. for 15 minutes. Place meatballs on a heating tray with a toothpick in each. Serve with a bowl of duck sauce.

(makes approximately 72 meatballs)

Punch

Scavenger Punch

3 pints cranberry juice cocktail
2 6-oz. cans frozen lemonade
2 c. water

2 oranges, sliced
2 bottles champagne

Mix all ingredients, omitting the champagne, in a punch bowl and add a ring of ice made by freezing water in a gelatin mold. Right before guests arrive, pour in the champagne.

(makes 32 4-oz. servings)

Dessert

Surprise Kabobs

pineapple (reserved from hors d'oeuvres and cut into chunks)
1 pint strawberries
1 11-oz. can mandarin oranges
2 bananas
1 8-oz. jar honey

maraschino cherries
grated coconut
lemon juice
wooden skewers

Peel bananas and slice into ½" slices. Dip in lemon juice so they don't turn color. Put fruit pieces on skewers alternating fruits. Dip half of skewered fruits in honey to cover and then into coconut. Lay fruits out on a round platter alternating coconut-covered and plain fruits.

(makes approximately 24 kabobs)

"Make Your Own" Sundaes

ice cream balls, assorted flavors   1 bowl hot fudge
1 bowl whipped cream   1 bowl sprinkles
1 bowl chopped nuts   maraschino cherries

Put all the above on a table and let everybody make their own creations.

"What's in the Box" Cake

1 package cake mix, any flavor   1 piece of cardboard 12" x 8"
1 can ready-made frosting (vanilla)   aluminum foil
1 tube cake decorating gel (brown)   black construction paper

Prepare cake mix according to package directions, using two 8" square pans. Let cakes cool. Frost as for a two-layer cake. Use cake decorating gel to make lines around edges of top corners of cake to give a box effect. Cover cardboard with aluminum foil. Cut the black construction paper into a 7" x 8" rectangle and glue to aluminum foil lining up the 8" edge with the cardboard edge. Make a slight fold where the black paper ends to tilt the cardboard. Put the foil below the black paper against the cake and press to stick. Put decorations on top of cake that look like Scavenger Hunt items. (Examples: small ball, artificial flowers, toy jewelry.) Serve with coffee and/or tea.

Special Activity

The surprise segment of the party will come at the end of the Scavenger Hunt. Everyone will meet at the home of one of the participants. There, the hostess will leave the cake, noisemakers, blowers and any other party paraphernalia desired. The hostess and guest of honor are the ones who make up the Scavenger Hunt and, consequently, they do not go out on the Hunt. They are needed at home to receive phone calls (which are part of the Scavenger Hunt). While everyone is out, the hostess can prepare for dessert. A schedule is very helpful for this party. Here is a sample:

1. Guests arrive. Have a cocktail hour serving the hors d'oeuvres and the punch. (1 hour)
2. Scavenger Hunt (1½ hours)
3. All the guests meet at a friend's house and return to hostess' house with the birthday cake and yelling "Surprise."
4. Go over items brought back from the Hunt and determine the winners (give out funny trophies to the winners and booby prizes to the losers). (1 hour)
5. Dessert, coffee and/or tea are served. (½ hour)
6. If all guests brought gifts, they can be opened. (½ hour)

The Scavenger Hunt

To organize the Scavenger Hunt, first separate guests into groups of two couples per car. Try to pair off two couples that are not very well acquainted with each other. This serves as an "ice breaker."

Make up enough Scavenger Hunt lists for each person. If you know someone who has access to a copying machine, it is a lot easier than making carbon copies. Make up a tally sheet with a column for each carload of people. State the assigned points for each acceptable item they obtain. Determine the winner by totaling the points. Along with the Scavenger Hunt lists, give out one paper bag per car. This bag is to be used for the items to be collected. Be sure everyone knows the time limit and any other limitations. When everyone has everything needed, they can all leave. Here is a sample Scavenger Hunt list.

SCAVENGER HUNT   SPONSORED BY (name)
READ EVERYTHING CAREFULLY BEFORE STARTING YOUR HUNT!
GOOD LUCK!

RULES: A.   No cheating
         B.   No bribery
         C.   No calls from LOCAL POLICE DEPT. for bail will
              be accepted
TOTAL EXPENSES: Not more than $1.00 per car
TIME ALLOWED: 1½ hours (9:30-11:00)
Winners will be decided on basis of points. Decisions of the judges are absolute!

	ITEMS	POINTS
1.	Last Year's Calendar	10
2.	Empty Beer Can	10
3.	A Menu from a Restaurant (name specific restaurant)	10
4.	A Key from a Motel Room	20
5.	Blue Matchbook	5
6.	Scorecard from Miniature Golf	20
7.	A Two-Dollar Bill	10
8.	A Program from a Sporting Event	25
9.	A Pencil from a Bowling Alley	15
10.	Roget's Thesaurus	10
11.	A White Flower	10
12.	An Application from a Tennis Club (name specific club)	10
13.	A Brown Shoelace	5
14.	A Piece of Waxed Paper from Pizza	10
15.	A Roller Skate Key	25
16.	1952 Penny	25
17.	A Road Map	5
18.	A Used Movie Ticket	10
19.	A Telephone Call from a Pay Telephone (give specific location and get the phone number of the phone beforehand to make sure the call comes from that phone)	15
20.	A Balloon with a String	10

TOTAL POINTS — 260

"All the world's a stage and all the men and women merely players"
— Shakespeare. This party gives everyone a chance to show that not all
the hams are in a food store.

Invitations

An emcee uses a microphone, therefore, the invitation can be made
in that shape.

1. Using 9" x 12" colored construction paper, fold in half lengthwise
   and then cut in half as in fig. 1.

fig. 1

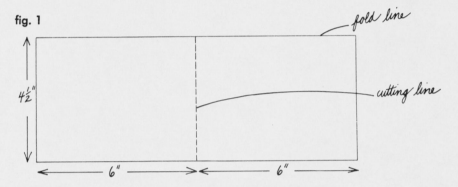

2. With fold on top, draw a microphone as in fig. 2.

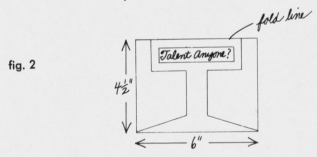

fig. 2

3. Cut around outline of microphone through both thicknesses and
   write on outside as shown in fig. 2.
4. On the inside write:

AUDITIONS BEING HELD FOR KRAZY TALENT SHOW
BIRTHDAY PARTY

AT: (name)
    (address)
DATE: (day and date)
TIME: (time)
RSVP BY: (date and telephone no.)

Decorations

Because this is a talent show, a stage area will be needed. An entranceway can be decorated as the performing area. Using streamers, drape them in the entranceway as in fig. 3.

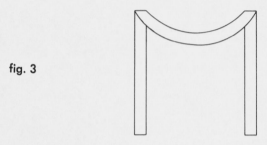

fig. 3

To make the streamers more decorative, do the following: Hold one streamer horizontally and place the end of another streamer on top vertically as shown in fig. 4 and tape in place.

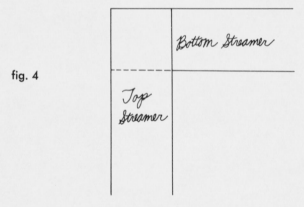

fig. 4

Take the horizontal piece and fold it to the left over the vertical piece. Now take the vertical streamer and bring it up and across the other streamer. Continue doing this until the streamer is the desired length. Be sure to keep untangling the streamer ends as you go.

Set up folding chairs in rows facing the stage area. Have card tables or other small tables around the room. Set up a small table with two chairs near the stage area for the judges. Put a bell on the table (it can be a dinner bell, cowbell, etc.). After the show, each guest should take a chair to one of the tables. Have on hand a movie camera so that motion pictures can be taken and shown at a future date.

Prepare a long table in a corner or on the side of the room for the hors d'oeuvres and dessert. Paper goods can be used for this party and can be placed on the buffet table beforehand.

Food

Hors d'Oeuvres

Krazy Balls

8 oz. shredded cheddar cheese
4 tbsp. melted butter
1¼ c. flour

¼ tsp. salt
1 tsp. paprika
36 stuffed green olives

Blend first five ingredients to form a dough. Mold 1 teaspoon of dough around each olive. Place on ungreased baking sheet. Cover to refrigerate or freeze if Krazy Balls are not to be used immediately. Bake 15 minutes at 400° F.

(makes 3 dozen)

Corny Pineapple

corned beef, sliced thin
pineapple chunks
Wrap each pineapple chunk with a slice of corned beef and secure with a toothpick. Bake at 350° F. for 10 to 15 minutes or until heated through.

Winning Spinach Quiche

3 tbsp. sweet butter
½ tsp. salt
½ tsp. paprika
3 tbsp. minced onion
1 10-oz. package frozen chopped spinach

4 eggs
¼ c. Jarlsberg or other mild cheese, grated
2 c. heavy cream
1 9″ pie shell, preheated

Cook spinach and drain. Sauté the onions in melted butter until soft. Add spinach. Mix in the salt and paprika. Cook until liquid is dissolved. Cool. Beat eggs and combine with cream. Add spinach and pour into the pie shell. Sprinkle the cheese on top. Bake at 375° F. for 30 minutes.

(serves 6 to 8)

Vegetable Prize Platter

cherry tomatoes
carrot sticks
celery sticks
cucumber spears
pepper sticks
ready-made dip

Lay out the vegetables on a round platter and put a bowl with the dip in the center.

Punch

Talented Punch

2 bottles club soda or ginger ale
1 large can pineapple juice
½ bottle vodka

1 pint lemon sherbet
orange slices
cherries

Make an ice ring by freezing water in a ring-shaped gelatin mold. Put ice in a punch bowl and add all the ingredients.

(makes approximately 30 4-oz. servings)

Dessert

"All the World's a Stage" Cake

1 package cake mix, any flavor
1 can ready-made frosting, any flavor
1 piece colored cardboard, 13" x 9"

Prepare cake mix according to package directions, using a 13" x 9" pan. Let cake cool. Frost cake. Cut out a hole in the cardboard as shown in fig. 5.

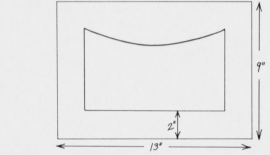

fig. 5

Put aluminum foil on the bottom 2" of the cardboard and press onto side of cake (see fig. 6). Decorate as shown. Serve cake with coffee and/or tea.

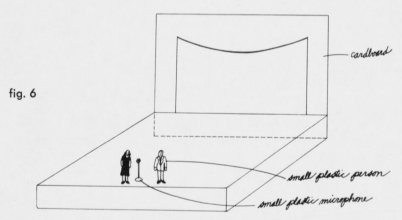

fig. 6

Special Activity

The whole fun of a Krazy Talent Show is to come up with the "kraziest" act and have lots of fun performing it. The host and hostess act as the organizers and emcees. Number slips of paper enough for one to each guest and put the slips in a fish bowl. As the guests arrive, have them pick a number. If they come as a couple, check to see if they have one act between the two of them. If they have one act, they take one number. While waiting for all the guests to arrive, conduct the cocktail hour. After the cocktail hour, the show can begin.

Have the guests take their seats and the judges take theirs. Of course, one of the judges is the emcee and should stand up and announce the first act. As the acts are going on, the judges should take the audience reaction into consideration when making a decision. If the act is really bad, give the people the courtesy of getting through most of their act; then ring the bell meaning "no good." Also have on hand props such as a large cane and a large butterfly net which can be used to pull the bad acts off the stage when they are "booed."

After all the acts are completed, the two judges have a conference and vote on the "kraziest" act. The emcee announces the winner and awards the prize (which should be a small gag gift).

Some people might have a bit of trouble thinking up "krazy" acts. We have, therefore, listed a few ideas.

Make up one costume that will attach two people together. Have them sing "Me and My Shadow."

Have someone put a paper bag with holes for eyes over his head and tell jokes.

Have someone do magic tricks in a Boy Scout uniform.

Have a male guest dress up in a ballet tutu and perform a ballet dance.

Have someone stand on his or her head and read poetry.

Have someone who doesn't know how to do birdcalls perform them.

COSTUME PARTY

"That's no lady, that's my husband," one of the authors of this book was heard to say to a passerby. Quickly, a 6'3", 220-lb. being clad in a housedress, stockings with knots around the calves, sneakers and a scarf around his head darted out of his car and into a costume birthday party. All sorts of weird creatures will attend your costume party. From the comic books to history and the stage and screen, your friends have the opportunity to be imaginative and high spirited.

Invitations

To give a hint as to the type of party you are giving, make the invitation a mask.

1. Use colored construction paper and cut a 6" x 7" rectangle. Fold the paper in half, making a rectangle 3½" x 6" (see fig. 1).

2. With the fold on top, round off the corners to form a mask, as in fig. 2.

3. Cut out holes for eyes through both thicknesses.

4. On the outside, write COSTUME BIRTHDAY PARTY.

5. On the inside write:
> DRESSING IN COSTUMES CAN BE LOTS OF FUN
> SO COME TO (name)'S HOUSE ON THE RUN.
> ADDRESS:
> DATE:
> TIME:
> RSVP BY: (date and phone number)

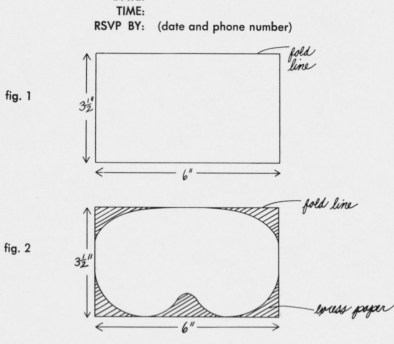

fig. 1

fig. 2

Decorations

Use streamers and balloons to make the room colorful. Hang up a "Happy Birthday" sign on a wall. No additional decorations are necessary, because the guests in their costumes add variety to the party room. A table can be placed in the corner or on a side of the room to use for hors d'ouevres and dessert. Paper plates, napkins and cups can be placed on the table.

Food

Hors d'Oeuvres

Masked Chicken Bits

4 chicken cutlets
1 egg
½ c. water
½ tsp. salt

3 tbsp. sesame seeds
½ c. flour
oil

Cut the chicken into 1" squares. Mix together the egg, water, salt, sesame seeds and flour. Heat the oil. Dip the chicken pieces in the batter and let the excess drip off. Fry 3 to 5 minutes or until golden brown. Serve with duck sauce for dipping.

(makes approximately 72 pieces)

Imaginative Noodle Pudding

1 8-oz. box medium noodles, cooked
½ stick butter
3 oz. cream cheese
½ c. sugar

3 eggs
1 c. milk
1 c. pineapple juice

Melt butter in small pot and pour into a 13" x 9" pan. Put the cooked noodles in the pan over the butter. With an electric mixer, mix the cream cheese and sugar together. Add the eggs. Mix thoroughly. Add the milk and the juice to the cheese mixture and pour over the noodles in the pan. The mixture in the pan will look very moist.

Topping: Mix together 1½ c. cornflake crumbs, ½ stick butter, 1 tsp. cinnamon and ¼ c. sugar. Sprinkle on top. Bake at 350° F. for 45 to 60 minutes. Let cool for 10 minutes before serving. This can be frozen after baking. Cut into 1" squares and put a toothpick in each.

(makes approx. 115 pieces)

Cheese and Crackers

Purchase an assortment of cheeses and crackers and serve on a large cheese board or platter.

Egg Rolls

Purchase frozen egg rolls, heat and serve with duck sauce.

Punch

Dressed-Up Punch

1 large can pineapple juice
¾ c. sugar
1 6-oz. can lemonade concentrate, frozen
2 c. water
1 quart strawberry ice cream
1 64-oz. bottle ginger ale

Defrost the lemonade. Mix the first four ingredients together in a punch bowl. Add an ice ring made by freezing water in a ring-shaped gelatin mold. Add ice cream and mix gently until blended. Add the ginger ale just before guests arrive.

(makes 35 4-oz. servings)

Dessert

Masquerade Cake

1 package cake mix, any flavor
2 cans ready-made frosting (1 vanilla and 1 chocolate)
   black string licorice

Prepare cake mix according to package directions, using a 13" x 9" pan. Let cake cool. Using a cup or glass with a 3" diameter top, gently press to mark two circles on the cake 2" from either 9" side and 3" down from the top. Cut as shown in fig. 3.

fig. 3

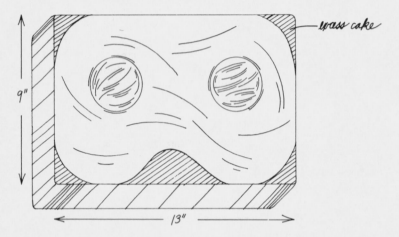

mass cake

9"

13"

Frost circles with chocolate frosting and the rest of the cake with vanilla. Put licorice on either side of the cake, pressing into the frosting on the sides (mask strings). Serve with coffee and/or tea.

Games

All Aboard!

The host or hostess and another person start this game. Everybody else leaves the room. The host or hostess is the conductor of the train. The conductor calls a guest into the room. The guest stands behind the conductor placing his or her hands on the conductor's waist.

Play starts with the host or hostess and the first person forming a line. They call in a third person who puts his hands on the waist of the one in front of him. The line has to alternate between male and female. The conductor says, "Choo-Choo, Choo-Choo" and shuffles around the room with everyone in line holding on. After a minute, the conductor stops, turns around and gives a passionate kiss to the next one in line who, in turn, turns around and gives a slap on the cheek to the third (last) person. Play continues with more guests joining the line as they are called into the room one by one, and with the last person in line getting slapped. The fun occurs when the line gets a little longer. The last person watches all the kisses getting passed and expects a kiss, but is quite surprised by the slap.

Trivia Game

Trivia is very popular and can be used as a game. Before the party, make up trivia questions relating to TV shows, movies or songs from your teenage years. Seat your guests comfortably and then begin asking them trivia questions. When someone knows the right answer, it can be called out. Give points for each correct answer and award a gag prize to the one who accumulates the most points.

Special Activity

The host or hostess can purchase inexpensive gag gifts or trophies and use them as prizes for the costumes. There should be two categories for prizes—funniest and most original. To vote on the costumes, give out a slip of paper and pencil to each guest and conduct a secret ballot. The ones who receive the most votes in each category are the winners.

When people call to RSVP and don't have any ideas for a costume, help them out. Some suggestions for costumes are: Prisoner and Catcher of Love (prisoner wears striped prison outfit with baseball attached to ankle by long chain and the Catcher wears a baseball catcher's uniform and holds the baseball), Little Red Riding Hood (red cape with a hood), boy and girl from the early 1900's, Hawaiian hula girl (grass skirt and lei), pair of dice (use two boxes with holes for head and arms and paint the boxes white with black dots).

CHAPTER VIII

Forty Years Old

The perfect wine, the perfect steak and perhaps the perfect being all improve with age. The statement, "You're not getting older, you're getting better," definitely applies as one nears his or her fortieth birthday.

Forty is the age where everything is within your grasp. One is not too young to rule the world; in the political arena, most of the high level victories are achieved after the fortieth year. One is not too old to throw a pass or make a slapshot, as professional athletes have proven.

To those who dreaded turning thirty and "died" with each successive year thereafter, upon the threshold of the fortieth birthday, life begins anew. With all that is ahead, the fortieth birthday is extremely significant and joyous. The experiences learned in your earlier years can now be relied upon to help carry you to greater heights and successes.

It is hard to remember your first birthday party so, if life begins at forty, happy first birthday.

THIS IS YOUR LIFE

This would make a good surprise party since, considering the theme, many old friends and those "long lost" relatives that you haven't kept in touch with should be contacted. It makes a nice reunion.

Invitations

A photo album reliving important events in one's life is nice to look through when friends and relatives get together. Make the invitation resemble an album.

1. Use colored construction paper 6¼" x 3½". Trim and draw a line down the middle as in fig. 1 to give a book appearance.

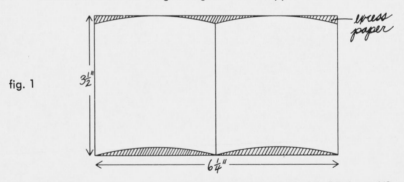

fig. 1

3½"

6¼"

press paper

2. On the left side, write: "YOU HAVE BEEN A PART OF (name)'S LIFE. PLEASE COME AND JOIN US ON A TRIP DOWN MEMORY LANE.

3. On the right side, write:

> DATE: (day and date)
> TIME:
> ADDRESS:
> RSVP BY: (date and phone number)

Decorations

Obtain baby pictures of the guest of honor and old pictures of people who will be attending the party. Have them blown up and hang them on the walls.

Set a long table with a linen cloth and have a seat for the guest of honor at the head of the table. Set another long table on the side of the room for hors d'oeuvres and dessert and lay out your dishes and silverware or use formal looking paper goods.

Food

Hors d'Oeuvres
Friendly Fondue

1 lb. Swiss cheese, grated
2 c. white wine
¼ c. cherry liqueur

2 loaves French bread, cut into cubes
1 clove garlic
pinches of salt, pepper and paprika

Rub the garlic clove on the inside of a fondue pot. Put wine in the pot and heat. When the wine bubbles, add cheese a handful at a time. When the cheese melts, add salt, pepper and paprika. Add the cherry liqueur while stirring constantly. Put the fondue pot out on the table with a bowl of cubed bread and fondue forks. To eat the fondue, put a cube of bread on a fondue fork and dip into the fondue.

Heavenly Stuffed Shells

1 12-oz. box jumbo macaroni shells   onion salt
    egg salad or shrimp salad (or any other salad)

Cook shells according to package directions, drain and let dry thoroughly on paper towels. In a deep fryer, fry six shells at a time until golden brown. Drain and sprinkle with onion salt. Cool and fill with salad.

(makes 40 to 45 hors d'oeuvres)

Pears With Ham

pear halves, each half sliced in two
prosciutto ham, sliced thin
Wrap pear in a slice of ham and secure with a toothpick.

Merry Stuffed Mushrooms

20 large mushrooms
¼ c. bread crumbs
  2 tbsp. onion, finely chopped

½ stick butter
  1 tbsp. Parmesan cheese
  butter

Wash mushrooms. Remove and save stems. Sauté onions in a small amount of butter until transparent. Chop stems. Melt ½ stick butter. Combine bread crumbs, onion, chopped stems and Parmesan cheese. Pour melted butter over mixture and mix well. Fill mushroom caps and place on cookie sheet. Bake at 350° F. for 20 minutes.

(makes 20 stuffed mushrooms)

Punch
Fruity Champagne
2 bottles pink champagne
1 pint raspberry sherbet

3 bananas, sliced
2 oranges, sliced

Mix all ingredients together and pour over ice in a punch bowl right before guests arrive.

(makes approximately 16 4-oz. servings)

Dessert
"Life is an Open Book" Cake
1 package cake mix, any flavor
1 can ready-made frosting (vanilla)
1 can ready-made frosting (chocolate)
1 tube cake decorating gel (brown)
Prepare cake mix according to package directions using a 13" x 9" pan. Let cake cool. Cut out as illustrated in fig. 2.

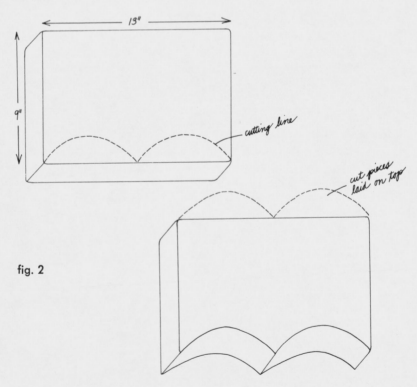

fig. 2

Frost top of cake with vanilla frosting. Frost sides of cake with chocolate frosting. Run tines of fork along sides of cake to give effect of pages in a book. Using gel, draw a line down the center of the cake and write "Happy Birthday." Serve with coffee and/or tea.

Games

Phrases of Yesteryear

Make up a slip of paper for each person with his name on it and a phrase or a word relating to the past of the guest of honor and each person. Give out the papers and have a guest relate a funny or not so funny story about the phrase or word on their paper. (*Examples:* Summer of '52 on the boardwalk, high school prom, camp)

Drop in the Bucket

Form two teams on one end of a room and line up behind a starting line. Have two buckets at the opposite end of the room, one opposite each team. Give the first two people on each team an inflated balloon and have them turn back to back and carry the balloon between their backs. They have to carry the balloon to the bucket and drop it in. After they drop the balloon in the bucket, the balloon is removed and the next couple can then start. If the balloon is dropped along the way, the couple returns to the starting line and starts over. The first team to finish is the winner.

Special Activity

When the guest of honor arrives, have only his close friends and relatives visible. In another room, have friends and relatives from the past waiting. One by one, have them say something to help the guest of honor identify them. After he succeeds or fails, have them come out and join the party. Do this until all the hidden people have made their appearance.

Collect photographs from friends and relatives of the guest of honor from infancy to the present and write witty captions for these pictures. Look through magazines (may be risqué if you choose) for cartoons for which funny captions can be made relating to the guest of honor. Put the photographs and cartoons along with the captions into a picture album. Have everyone sit in a semicircle around the guest of honor and he or she can read the captions under each picture and hold them up for all to see. This can be quite amusing if you use ingenuity and creativity when making up the captions.

MYSTERY BUS RIDE

"I wonder where we're going?" The fun of a Mystery Bus Ride is that the destination is kept a secret. This is a unique party and one your guests will surely remember.

Invitations

1. Using a sheet of 9" x 12" construction paper, fold in half lengthwise and cut the folded paper in two (see fig. 1).

fig. 1

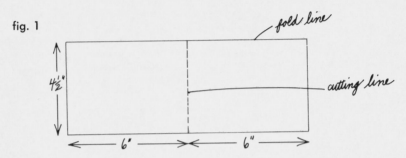

2. With the fold on the left side, write: WHERE ARE WE GOING? THAT'S FOR ME TO KNOW AND FOR YOU TO FIND OUT.
3. Open it up and on the inside write: PLEASE MEET US AT THE PARKING LOT AT (address) ON (day and date) AT (time). WE WILL BE TAKING A MYSTERY BUS RIDE IN HONOR OF (name)'S BIRTHDAY. NOBODY KNOWS WHERE WE ARE GOING!!!
   RSVP BY: (date and phone number)

Decorations

Make up large question marks from oak tag paper and hang them on the walls. Road maps and pictures of local points of interest add a nice touch also.

Set up a long table on the side or in a corner of the room for hors d'oeuvres and dessert. Hang streamers and balloons above the table. A "Happy Birthday" sign can be hung on the wall over the table. Use a bright-colored tablecloth with matching paper goods. Card tables with tablecloths matching the hors d'oeuvres table can be set up around the room.

Food

Hors d'Oeuvres

Mystery Kabobs

½ c. sherry	½ c. honey	1 tsp. ground ginger
1 c. soy sauce	¼ c. oil	1 tsp. garlic powder

Combine all of the above ingredients for a marinade.

2½ lbs. beef, cubed	1 pint cherry tomatoes
½ lb. bag pearl onions	1 large can pineapple chunks

Marinate the beef for several hours in the above marinade. Place the beef, onions, tomatoes and pineapple chunks on skewers and broil.

(makes approximately 16 servings)

Surprise Rice

¼ c. chopped green pepper
1 c. chopped celery
¼ c. chopped onion
½ stick butter
2 tbsp. frozen orange juice concentrate

1¼ c. water
½ tsp. salt
1⅓ c. rice, uncooked
1 small can miniature shrimp, drained

In a large skillet, sauté green pepper, celery and onion in butter until tender. Stir in orange juice, water and salt. Bring to boil. Add rice and continue cooking as directed on package. Stir in shrimp.

(makes 10 ½-cup servings)

Mysterious Asparagus

1 fresh white bread, sliced thin (crust removed)
1 can asparagus spears
1 stick sweet butter, softened
Parmesan cheese

Roll bread slice flat with a rolling pin. Put asparagus spear in center and roll it up. Cut in half. Melt butter. Dip roll in melted butter and in Parmesan cheese to coat. Bake at 350° F. for 30 minutes. May be frozen before baking.

(makes approximately 15 hors d'oeuvres)

Salmon Wheels

3 slices smoked salmon, minced
3 oz. cream cheese
¼ tsp. Worcestershire sauce
1 tsp. chopped chives

parsley
2 cucumbers, sliced
stuffed green olives, sliced

Combine salmon and cream cheese. Add Worcestershire sauce and chives. Place one teaspoon of mixture on each cucumber slice. Sprinkle with parsley flakes and top with an olive slice. Refrigerate until serving time.

(makes approximately 2 dozen hors d'oeuvres)

Punch

Hunch Punch

2 bottles ginger ale
1 large can pineapple juice
½ bottle vodka

1 pint strawberries
2 oranges, sliced

Prepare a ring of ice for the punch bowl by freezing water in a ring-shaped gelatin mold. Combine all the above ingredients and pour over the ice ring in a punch bowl.

(makes approximately 35 4-oz. servings)

Dessert

"Where To?" Cake

1 package cake mix, any flavor
1 can ready-made frosting (vanilla)
1 tube cake decorating gel (brown)

Prepare cake mix according to package directions using two 9" round pans. Let cakes cool. Cut both layers as shown in fig. 2.

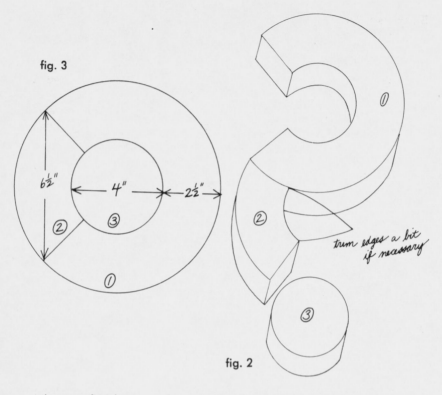

fig. 3

fig. 2

trim edges a bit
if necessary

Arrange first layer as shown in fig. 3. and frost. Lay pieces for second layer on top and frost entire cake.

Use gel to outline edges of question mark. Serve with coffee and/or tea.

Special Activity

For this party you will have to make arrangements to charter a bus for the evening. Naturally, this can run into a bit of money and should be checked into before deciding on a bus company.

To start off a Mystery Bus Ride, have everyone meet in a parking lot near your home. Try to find a parking lot that is not being used on the night of your party so it will not be too crowded. Have your guests park near the bus. When everyone has arrived, you may embark on your trip. Take along bottles of champagne and disposable champagne glasses, chips and other snack foods. Have the bus driver drive around for about an hour on dark, curved roads. Let him stop at a local cemetery, prison or city hall and pretend that it is your destination. He can also point out anything interesting along the way. After driving for quite a while, have the bus driver drive to your home. When the bus arrives at your house, have everyone come inside. Have the bus wait outside during the party to take everyone back to the parking lot (if the bus is hired for the evening and not by the hour). Otherwise, the people can be driven to the parking lot.

Another way to conduct this type of party is to have the bus take everyone to a restaurant. Plans have to be made with the restaurant beforehand so that they will be expecting your group.

GAME NIGHT

Games are very popular nowadays, with many new games constantly coming on the scene. The game manufacturers seem to be catering more than ever before to the adult market, with many interesting games to choose from. A Game Night is a way for people to come together socially, play their favorite games and celebrate the birthday of a friend or relative.

Invitations

1. Using 9" x 12" colored construction paper, fold in half widthwise.
2. Cut the folded paper in half as in fig. 1.

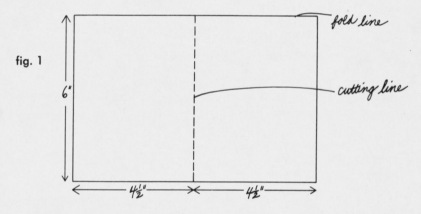

fig. 1

3. With the fold on top, write a large "40" on the front with one of the following drawn in each of the four corners: heart, spade, diamond and club.
4. On the inside, write the following:

fig. 2

Scrabble®, bridge, Monopoly® and more —
Come and play the games galore!!
                    RSVP BY: (date and phone number)
When people RSVP, ask them to name their favorite games to give you
an idea of the games to be played.

Decorations

Set up card tables around the room. There are paper tablecloths
available with a playing card motif which could be used for the card
tables. Put a long table on the side or in the corner of the room for hors
d'oeuvres and dessert.

Set the games up around the room. Have a dictionary and the rules
for the games available. As an added touch, make up your own game
rules and write them on large sheets of paper and hang them on the
walls. Large playing cards can be hung on the walls.

Food

Hors d'Oeuvres
Heart Sandwiches

bread slices   luncheon meats   cherry tomatoes
Using heart-shaped cookie or canapé cutters, cut hearts in the bread and
luncheon meat. Make open-faced sandwiches and top each with half a
cherry tomato and secure with a toothpick.

Scrabble® Rolls

1 6½-oz. can salmon   1 tsp. instant minced onion
1 3-oz. can chopped mushrooms   ¼ c. mayonnaise
¼ c. celery, chopped fine   4 hard rolls
Mix first five ingredients. Cut tops off the rolls and scoop out the centers.
Fill the rolls with the salmon.   (makes 4 servings)

Chinese Checker Rollups

½ lb. ground beef   1 envelope onion soup mix
1 c. bean sprouts, drained   1 egg
½ c. water chestnuts, chopped   12 large lettuce leaves
1 4-oz. can mushrooms, drained and chopped
Brown first six ingredients in a skillet. Stuff the lettuce leaves with the
mixture and secure with a toothpick.   (makes 12 servings)

Winning Tuna Ball

2 c. tuna   ¼ tsp. salt
8 oz. cream cheese, softened   ½ c. walnuts, chopped
1 tbsp. lemon juice   3 tbsp. parsley
2 tsp. minced onion   green olives
1 tsp. horseradish

Drain and flake tuna. Combine with the next five ingredients. Form a ball and roll in mixture of walnuts and parsley. Decorate with green olives and chill.

(makes 40 to 50 servings)

Punch

Game Night Punch

2 quarts cranberry juice cocktail   1 quart club soda
2 quarts orange juice   2 oranges, sliced
Make an ice ring by freezing water in a ring-shaped gelatin mold and pour all the above ingredients over the ice in a punch bowl.

(makes 40 4-oz. servings)

Dessert

Dice Cake

2 packages cake mix, any flavor   chocolate covered mints
2 cans ready-made frosting (vanilla)
Prepare the two packages cake mix according to package directions using four 8" square pans. Let cakes cool. Make two two-layer cakes frosted with the vanilla frosting. Use chocolate covered mints for the spots on the dice. Put one in the middle of one cake and lay three diagonally across the top of the second cake. Serve with coffee and/or tea.

Games and Special Activity

Rotating Tables

Before the guests arrive, the games can be set up at the tables. Instead of having your guests play only one game for the evening, they can rotate from one table to another at ½-hour intervals. When planning the games to be played, be sure they are short enough so that, after a half hour, people can stop and move to another game. (Examples: card games, backgammon, Rummy-Q, checkers, word games)

Group Games

Another alternative is to set up one long table for everyone to sit at and play games as a group. (Examples: Bingo,® Michigan Rummy, Po-Ke-No®)

"Las Vegas" Night

For this type of game night, set up tables with different games played in Las Vegas. (Examples: blackjack, roulette, poker)

"Bring Your Own Game" Night

This type of party is good for a small group of people. Have each couple bring a game. Everyone is given the opportunity to learn and play a new and different game that has been brought by someone else.

WINES AND CHEESES OF THE WORLD

The Book of Ecclesiastes in the Bible says, "Eat thy bread with joy and drink thy wine with a merry heart . . ." A wine-tasting party is lots of fun and gives people an opportunity to sample new and unusual wines and cheeses in addition to celebrating the birthday of a friend or relative.

Invitations

1. Using 9" x 12" red construction paper, fold in half lengthwise.
2. Use the lid from a ½-pound tub of margarine as a pattern for a 4"-diameter circle and draw it onto the folded construction paper with a small segment of the circle on the fold (see fig. 1).

fig. 1

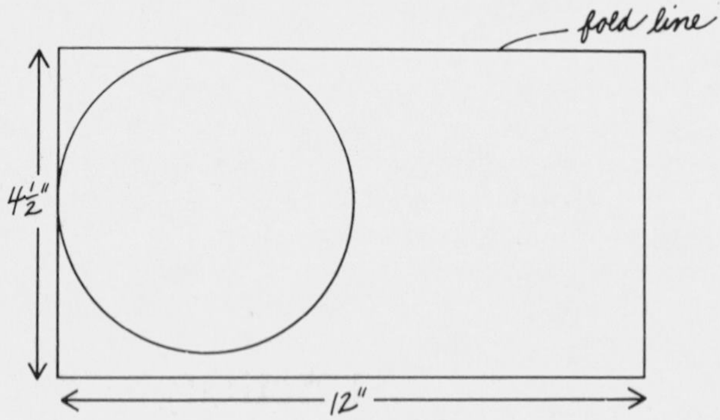

3. Cut out the circle, leaving a segment of it attached at the fold line.
4. On the outside, write: PLEASE COME AND HAVE A "GOUDA" TIME — — —
5. On the inside write:
   AT A WINE AND CHEESE TASTING PARTY — — —
   FOR: (name)
   WINE CELLAR: (address)
   GRAPE SQUEEZING DATE: (day and date)
   TASTING TIME: (time)
   RSVP BY: (date and phone number)

Decorations

Decorations can be kept simple. Set up two long tables for the wines, cheeses and bread. Hang a "Happy Birthday" sign over the tables. Use red, white and yellow as the color scheme of the party to go along with the colors of the wines and cheeses. Use white tablecloths on the tables and put red paper plates and napkins on the table. Some yellow streamers (with holes punched in them to simulate Swiss cheese) and balloons can be hung around the room.

Food

Cheese

For the cheeses, you can go into cheese specialty shops or gourmet shops and find a large selection. Purchase a nice variety of mild cheeses (the salespeople are very helpful when selecting cheeses and deciding on quantities needed). Be sure to have the names of the cheeses marked on the packages so you will know which is which. Some of the better known mild cheeses are Jarlsberg, Gouda, Havarti, Fontina and Muenster. The cheeses should be stored in the refrigerator until party time and wrapped as air-tight as possible. Take out of the refrigerator one hour before serving, since cheese should be served at room temperature to best enjoy its flavor.

Wine

The wines can be purchased in a wine shop or package goods store. The salespeople in these shops are very accommodating and will help you choose a nice variety of red and white wines. In order to judge how much wine will be necessary, figure on ½-¾ of a bottle per person. As an aid when choosing wines, here are some of the major wine producing countries and the wines they are famous for: Italy-Chianti (red), Germany-Liebfraumilch (white), France-Sauternes (white) and Burgundy (red), United States-Cabernet Sauvignon (red), Switzerland-Fendant de Sion (white), Austria-Grinzinger (white) and Greece-Mavrodaphne (red).

Dessert
International Cake

1 package cake mix, any flavor
2 cans ready-made frosting (vanilla)
   green food coloring
   blue food coloring
   pastry bag

Prepare cake mix according to package directions using two 9" round pans or two 2-quart casserole bowls. For the casserole, allow extra baking time and test cake as directed on package. Let cakes cool. Using an atlas or any other book with maps, find pictures of the eastern and western hemispheres that can fit on top of the two 9" round cakes or casseroles. Trace them onto waxed paper using the point of a pencil to mark the lines on the paper. Lay the waxed paper on top of the unfrosted cake and push a toothpick through the waxed paper on the lines to make an outline on the cake. Repeat this for the second cake (you will have one hemisphere outlined on each cake). The maps can be drawn on the waxed paper freehand instead of being traced. Using ½-can vanilla frosting, tint it green with food coloring. Put frosting in pastry bag and go around outlines with the frosting and fill in the landmasses. Tint the remaining 1½ cans of vanilla frosting blue and frost the rest of the cakes with a spatula or knife to look like water. Lay the two cakes, sides touching, on a piece of cardboard covered with aluminum foil (see fig. 2).

fig. 2

Special Activity

To prepare for the wine and cheese tasting party, make up a paper listing the wines and cheeses being served for each of the guests. Leave space next to each for comments. These papers can be taken home so your guests have a record of the wines and cheeses they enjoyed. When making up the wine list, white wines should be first and then red wines. Make up small flags and glue to toothpicks. Write the cheese names on the flags.

One hour before the party, cut loaves of French bread and the cheeses into cubes. Keep each type of cheese on a separate plate and put a flag in each cheese. Spread the plates of cheeses and bread out across the two long tables. Have a pitcher of water on the table to use for rinsing out the wineglasses and a receptacle for the water after the glasses are rinsed. Be sure to have enough wineglasses for everyone.

The red wines can be opened and placed on the table. The white wines should be kept chilled until party time. Right before your guests arrive, take the white wines out of the refrigerator and line them up on the table with the red wines. The wines should be in the same order as they are listed on the papers made up for the guests.

For wine tasting, all that is necessary is one to two ounces of wine in a glass. There are three characteristics to consider when judging wine. The first characteristic is the color. Hold your glass of wine up to the light and look at it. The wine should be clear. After you have admired the clarity of the wine, swirl it around gently to release the full aroma (bouquet) of the wine. People get great pleasure from sniffing the bouquet of a good-tasting wine, for sniffing a good wine is the next best thing to tasting it. After enjoying the aroma, take a sip of the wine. Hold it in your mouth for a few seconds and swish it around your tongue to get the full flavor. Having fully enjoyed (or maybe not so fully enjoyed) your glass of wine, write down your comments.

The cheeses and breads placed on the tables are for nibbling between tasting the wines. They wipe away the taste of wine and prepare your mouth for its next sensation. The wineglasses should be rinsed between tastes so that there is no residue from the previous wine in your glass.

After all the wines and cheeses have been sampled, seconds are in order. Go ahead, enjoy yourself and refill your glass once, twice or three times. When everyone is ready for dessert, sherbet can be served as an "intermezzo." A flavorful finale to this unique evening is birthday cake served with coffee and/or tea.

CHAPTER IX

60 Years Old and Over

Congratulations to whomever will be celebrating a 60+ birthday. Before making plans for the birthday party, stop and think a while of the accomplishment of the birthday person. Achieving this age is in itself a most important reason to celebrate.

At the turn of the twentieth century, reaching the age of 60 was not very common. Life expectancy was shorter and life itself was more difficult to sustain. Today the birthday person and our society have come a long way. In a sense, the sixtieth birthday is considered by many people their first, as they are opening up new doors and beginning new lives while entering or looking towards retirement. It is a time when dreams and plans of the future become the present and one lives through the years of doing what he "always wanted to do."

Birthday parties for people sixty years old and over are well earned and deserve commemoration. It is important to show these "youngsters" love, affection and appreciation through a sincere birthday bash.

A grandma of seventeen children was given a surprise birthday party by her daughter-in-law. The party was an unqualified success, because among the partygoers were about a dozen children around the age of five. Grandma's birthday coincided with one of her granddaughter's and, therefore, the surprise party was for both of them. The joy and warmth was only exceeded by all the fun that both birthday girls had at this mixed birthday. It was a sight to behold, watching granddaughter and grandmother play all the games together, share a cake and wear the same birthday hats.

Let's break out the candles, the cake and the confetti — Happy Birthday 60+!

SOCIAL SECURITY

Becoming Social Security age and entering retirement are both good reasons to celebrate one's birthday. Any age deserves celebration, but the above is one of those milestone ages.

Invitations

A Social Security card makes a perfect invitation for this party. You can send everyone an enlarged card.

1. Using a 3" x 5" white index card, draw a ¼" border around all four edges with a light blue fine-tip marking pen.
2. Write the following on the card:

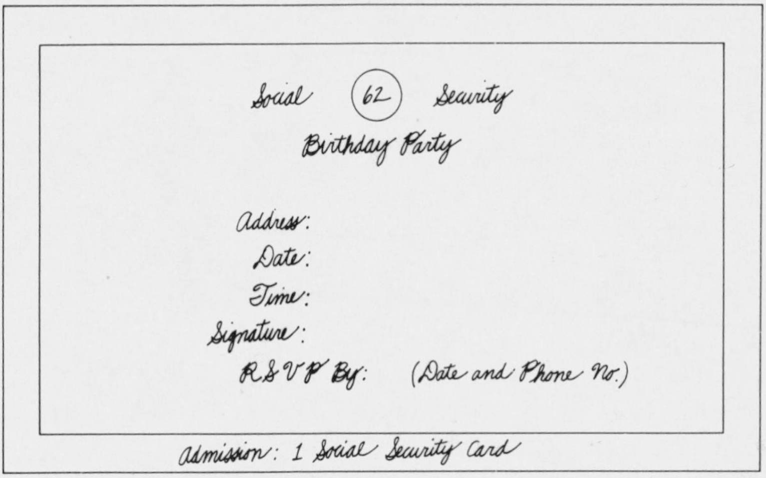

Social (62) Security
Birthday Party

Address:
Date:
Time:
Signature:
R S V P By: (Date and Phone No.)

Admission: 1 Social Security Card

fig. 1

Decorations

Because a Social Security card is light blue and white, the color scheme should be these colors. The room can be set up like a ballroom, with small round tables along the walls and a dancing area in the middle. Use white tablecloths for the tables. If possible, put a long table for hors d'oeuvres and dessert in a separate room. Lay out blue paper plates, cups and napkins or, if you happen to have blue dishes, use them.

In the center of the dance floor, hang a cluster of blue-and-white balloons from the ceiling. They can be intertwined with streamers. Drape blue-and-white streamers from the center of the ceiling over the dance floor outward.

Food

Hors d'Oeuvres
Social Security Spread

¼ c. crushed pineapple
½ c. chicken, cooked and minced
3 tbsp. mayonnaise
French dressing

Marinate chicken in dressing about one hour. Drain pineapple; save the liquid. Mix all ingredients, using pineapple juice to bring to spreading consistency. Serve with onion melba toast.

Golden Cauliflower

1 c. flour
½ tsp. salt
1 c. beer
1 tsp. baking powder
2 eggs
½ c. salad oil
¼ tsp. pepper
¾ c. water
flour
cauliflower
oil

Cut cauliflower into pieces. Make sure the cauliflower is dry before dipping into batter. Heat oil in a deep fryer to 375° F. Beat first eight ingredients until smooth. Coat cauliflower with flour and dip into batter. Fry until golden brown. Drain.

"Prime" Roast Beef

Prepare a roast of beef and slice thin. Put on a platter decorated with parsley and cherry tomatoes. Serve with small dinner rolls.

Dancing Stuffed Cabbage

2 heads cabbage
3 jars chili sauce
3 large cans jellied cranberry sauce
2 lbs. ground beef

¼ c. uncooked rice
salt
pepper
raisins (optional)

Combine ground beef, rice, dash salt and dash pepper. Boil water in a large pot. In a second large pot, combine chili sauce and cranberry sauce. Heat until the cranberry sauce is melted. Add raisins to sauce, if desired. In the boiling water, cook the cabbage heads until the leaves are softened (about 15 minutes). Remove the cabbage from the water and let drain. Place 2 tablespoons of meat in a cabbage leaf at the core end of the leaf. Roll the end of the cabbage leaf over the meat just to cover. Fold in the two sides (flaps) and then roll up completely. After all the meat and cabbage are used, gently place the rolled cabbage in the pot of sauce. Cook on a low to medium heat for 1 hour.

(makes approximately 30 hors d'oeuvres)

Punch

Retirement Punch

1 gallon sangria
  apples, sliced
  oranges, sliced

bananas, sliced
strawberries, sliced

Prepare an ice ring by freezing water with maraschino cherries in it in a ring-shaped gelatin mold. Combine all ingredients in a punch bowl and add ice.

(makes approximately 32 4-oz. servings)

Dessert

"Social Security Card" Cake

1 package cake mix, any flavor
1 can ready-made frosting (vanilla)
1 tube cake decorating gel, blue

Prepare cake mix according to package directions, using a 13" x 9" pan. Let cake cool. Frost with vanilla frosting, making the frosting smooth by dipping a spatula in warm water and smoothing it out. Use gel to draw a border line around the cake. For the writing on the cake, use a toothpick to mark frosting before using the gel (to avoid mistakes). Write on the cake as shown in fig. 2.

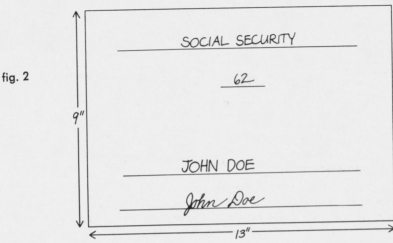

fig. 2

9"

13"

SOCIAL SECURITY

62

JOHN DOE

John Doe

Games

Social Security Poker

For this game, everyone has to take out his or her Social Security card. Guests study their numbers to find the best poker hands they can (the zeroes are used as tens). The one with the best hand is the winner and can be given a gag gift. In novelty stores you can find a roll of toilet tissue with fake money printed on it, a large dollar bill or play money.

Change Your Partners

Put some music on and get your guests to dance. When the first piece is over, everyone splits up and the women pick a new partner on the dance floor. They dance together for the second song and, when the music stops, the men pick a new partner for the third dance. Continue doing this, alternating the songs and who picks the partners. See Special Activity for the music to be played.

Special Activity

Think back to when you were a teenager and enjoyed dancing with your friends. What dances did you do? Over the decades, the dances have changed along with the teenagers. It can be lots of fun to "dance" through the generations. A bit of research will be necessary. To find out what dances were popular and how to do them, you can go to the library or ask someone who was a teenager in a particular decade to show you the dance. Also, many libraries lend out records which will enable you to obtain music from the various decades. The following is a list of some of the more popular dances from each decade.

1920-1930	Charleston
1930-1940	Conga, Big Apple, Lindy

1940-1950	Jitterbug, Lindy
1950-1960	Bop, Stroll, Slop
1960-1970	Twist, Swim, Monkey
1970-1980	Hustle, Bump

LOOKING BACK TO THE GOOD OLD DAYS

Reminiscing with relatives and old friends is always enjoyable. By using the "good old days" as a theme, you can bring back those delightful memories.

Invitations

There must be times when you have caught yourself daydreaming about the past and some of those fond memories. A cloud as an invitation can symbolize those reflections on the past.

1. Using 9" x 12" white construction paper, fold in half widthwise and cut in half as in fig. 1.

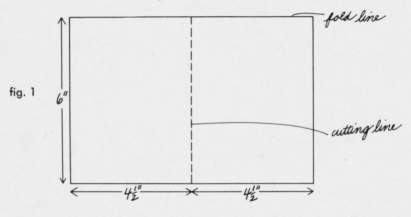

fig. 1

2. With the fold on the left, cut out a cloud shape similar to fig. 2.

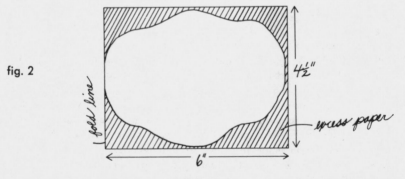

fig. 2

3. On the outside write: REMEMBER THE GOOD OLD DAYS WHEN YOU WERE A TEENAGER?

4. Open up the invitation and write:
   DRESS AS YOU DID WHEN YOU WERE A TEEN
   A BIRTHDAY PARTY AT (name)'S HOUSE IS THE SCENE.
   PLACE: (address)
   DATE: (day and date)
   FOR: (name)
   RSVP BY: (date and phone number)

Decorations

A "Happy Birthday" sign can be hung on a wall. Hang thin string from one side of a room to the other, making straight lines across the room. Every so often, hang a cluster of colorful balloons on the strings. Set up a long table in a corner or side of the room for hors d'oeuvres and dessert. A decorative paper tablecloth should be used on the table and the paper goods should match the tablecloth.

The decorations should reflect age groups of the partygoers. Large pictures of clothes, people and events of their time can be hung on the walls. All the guests will be wearing "costumes" from their teenage years. For further details, see Special Activity.

Food

Hors d'Oeuvres
Cheese Lollipops
8 oz. cream cheese, softened   ½ tsp. Worcestershire sauce
½ c. finely grated cheddar cheese   pretzel sticks
½ envelope onion soup mix
Combine cream cheese with cheddar cheese. Mix in Worcestershire sauce and onion soup mix. Crush pretzel sticks. Roll cheese mixture into small balls and roll in pretzel crumbs. Place a pretzel stick in the middle as a toothpick.

(makes 30 to 40 servings)

Banana Wraps
8 medium bananas, peeled   2 tsp. sugar
⅓ c. soy sauce   20 slices bacon, cut in half
Cut bananas in 1" chunks. Pour soy sauce and sugar mixture over bananas. Marinate 30 minutes. Wrap each banana chunk in ½ slice of bacon. Broil 4" from heat for about 7 minutes or until browned.

(makes approximately 40 hors d'oeuvres)

Teen Tuna Spread
1 envelope unflavored gelatin   ⅓ c. mayonnaise
1 can tomato soup   ½ c. chopped celery
⅔ c. milk   ½ onion, chopped
6 oz. cream cheese, softened   2 6½-oz. cans tuna

Dissolve gelatin in the milk. Heat the tomato soup and cream cheese until smooth. Add the gelatin and milk mixture and fold in the mayonnaise. Mix the celery, onion and tuna in a bowl and add to the mixture. Put in a one-quart mold and chill. Serve with crackers.

Peppy Pepper Steak

1½ lbs. shoulder steak, cut into strips
1 onion
3 peppers, cut into strips
  oil
2 beef bouillon cubes
1 tbsp. cornstarch
2 tbsp. soy sauce
1 tsp. sugar
1 can Chinese vegetables
1 c. boiling water
white rice, cooked

Sauté onions and peppers in a little oil until tender. Remove and in the same pan brown the meat quickly. Add peppers. Dissolve bouillon cubes in boiling water and add to pan. Mix cornstarch, soy sauce and sugar together and add to the mixture in the pan. Add vegetables. Simmer about 45 minutes or until meat is tender. Serve over white rice.

(makes approximately 8 servings)

Punch

Lively Generation Punch

2 6-oz. cans frozen lemonade concentrate
2 6-oz. cans frozen orange juice concentrate
2 quarts water
1 28-oz. bottle Seven-Up lemon-lime soda
1 pint orange sherbet

Prepare an ice ring by freezing water in a ring-shaped gelatin mold. Pour above ingredients over ice ring in a punch bowl and serve.

(makes approximately 30 4-oz. servings)

Dessert

"Looking Back" Cake

1 package cake mix, any flavor
1 can ready-made frosting (vanilla)
1 tube cake decorating gel (brown)

Prepare cake mix according to package directions, using two 8" or 9" round pans. Frost as for two-layer cake. With gel, write every decade of the birthday person's life in place of the numbers on a clock. Point the big hand to the current decade and the small hand to the teenage decade (see fig. 3).

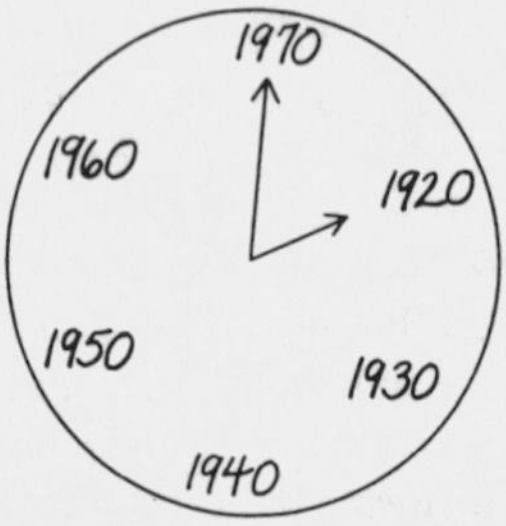

fig. 3

Special Activity

When guests call to RSVP, tell them to come to the party dressed in the type of clothing worn in the birthday person's teenage years. Most likely it will be the same dress as when they were teenagers. For example, in the 1920's females wore low-waisted dresses and males wore baggy trousers and argyle vests. Raccoon coats were also very popular. The Charleston was the dance craze of the time.

Many libraries have records from the past that can be borrowed and used for the party. Otherwise, you can invest in one or two records with music from the era. You might also be able to procure some of the past music by asking some of your friends.

It can be loads of fun bringing back those good old days and acting like a teenager again.

COCKTAIL HOUR AND BUFFET

When in the mood to make a really formal birthday party, a cocktail hour and buffet can fill the bill. It provides an opportunity to bring out all your best table linens, china and silverware and to have all your friends concentrated in one area — your home.

Invitations

1. Purchase formal note cards.
2. On the card write the following:

MR. AND MRS. (name)
REQUEST THE PLEASURE OF YOUR COMPANY
AT A BIRTHDAY COCKTAIL HOUR AND BUFFET
IN HONOR OF (name)
ON (date) AT HOME AT (time)
RSVP   (date and phone number)

Decorations

For this party, decorate with a formal atmosphere. Set up a long table for hors d'oeuvres and dessert, preferably in a dining room or kitchen, using a linen tablecloth and matching napkins. Have a separate table for beverages. Take out your fine china and good silverware and really go overboard. Purchase fresh flowers to use as a centerpiece on the hors d'oeuvres table or, if you have an arrangement of dried or artificial flowers, it can be used.

Arrange the food around the table in an orderly fashion, starting with plates, silverware and napkins. Next lay out the main course with serving pieces. The salad can be at the end with an assortment of dressings within reach or a "house" dressing already on the salad. Have small tables strategically placed around the room on which people can rest their food and drinks. Hang a "Happy Birthday" sign in the entranceway to the party room or over the buffet table.

Food

Creamy Shrimp Dip

8-oz. container whipped cream cheese
2 jars cocktail shrimp (in sauce)   parsley or finely chopped nuts
1 tsp. lemon juice   1 green pepper

Mix the first three ingredients together. Scoop out the pepper and stuff with the shrimp mixture. Sprinkle with parsley or nuts. Serve with potato chips or crackers.

Cocktail Tree

cherry tomatoes	cheese chunks	smoked oysters
olives	turkey cubes	sweet pickles
pineapple chunks	shrimp	

Put the above ingredients on toothpicks and push into a 12" plastic foam cone.

Brisket with Noodles

3 lb. beef brisket   2 tbsp. celery flakes
2 tbsp. vinegar   1 can tomato soup
2 tbsp. sugar   8 oz. ketchup
1 tsp. salt   2 tbsp. brown sugar
4 whole cloves   2 tbsp. lemon juice
1 bay leaf   cooked wide noodles
⅛ tsp. instant minced garlic

Put meat in a large pot with enough hot water to cover. Add vinegar, sugar, salt, cloves, bay leaf, garlic and celery flakes to water. Simmer covered for 3 hours. Mix tomato soup, ketchup, brown sugar and lemon juice. Slice meat and add to mixture. Cover and bake at 300° F. for 1 hour. Serve over noodles.   (makes approximately 10 servings)

Prepare a tossed salad with your favorite dressing or put out a selection of dressings. Dinner rolls and/or bread can be placed on the table.

Watermelon Bowl

Cut a watermelon in half lengthwise, scoop out the fruit and cut the edge to make a decorative border. Put fresh or canned fruit and the watermelon into the shell. If desired, add 1 cup of Amaretto and mix gently.

Fancy Butter Cookies

½ lb. sweet butter, softened   2½ c. flour
⅔ c. sugar   sprinkles, coconut or chopped nuts
3 egg yolks   ready-made frosting (chocolate)
1 tsp. vanilla

Combine butter, sugar, egg yolks and vanilla. Mix thoroughly. Work in the flour with hands. Fill cookie press with dough. Form cookies onto ungreased baking sheet. Bake at 375° F. for 7 to 10 minutes until set. Cool. Put frosting between two cookies, forming a sandwich and roll edges in sprinkles, coconut or nuts.   (makes 3 dozen)

Birthday Cake

Prepare a round cake. Frost and decorate it according to your own creative desires.

Special Activity

A cocktail party is a good opportunity to invite a large group of people with a variety of backgrounds. Since many of the people might not be acquainted with one another, being prepared with some "ice breakers" might add to the success of the party.

When your guests arrive and their wraps, if any, are removed, introductions are in order. When you have a large group, introduce any people who are complete strangers to one or two other couples. When the introduction is made, mention something personal about each individual so that guests will have a topic of conversation to start with. Games are another way for people to interact.

Opposites Attract

Before the party, prepare cards by attaching strings so that they can be worn around the neck. Write words that are opposites on the cards. (*Examples:* hot-cold, weak-strong, black-white, big-small, high-low, up-down, dirty-clean and dark-light). As each guest arrives, he picks a card from a bag and hangs it around his neck. The object of the game is to find the person with the opposite word and to introduce oneself.

What Am I?

Prepare pieces of paper with the names of different objects. As your guests arrive, pin one of the papers an each one's back. The object of the game is to guess what you are by asking the other guests questions. The answers can only be "yes" or "no." While you are asking questions, the other guests are doing the same, thus everyone is conversing. Examples of objects are: TV, radio, chair, table, refrigerator, bed.

Sentence Scramble

Before the party, prepare a few sentences. Write one word of the sentence on a card. Use enough cards to complete the sentences. Attach a string to each card so it can be worn around the neck. As each guest arrives, put a card around his neck and give him a piece of paper and a pencil. Each guest should try to form a sentence with the word on his card by looking for other people with words that go along with his to form a sentence. The sentence does not have to be long. As a sentence is formed, write it down and go on to create another sentence with other words (people). Examples of sentences are: The boy ran away; Stop and look; This is blue; Go buy a newspaper for me; Roses are red.

CHAPTER X

One Hundred Years Old

Consider the accomplishment of living to be one hundred. A century is a life that has spanned many generations; a life through which the world has changed and changed. It is a life through which one has seen, learned and contributed much. One hundred — that's triple the life expectancy in many nations throughout the world.

When becoming a centenarian, one does not celebrate a birthday, one commemorates an event that all too few people have the opportunity to enjoy. This most exclusive club should welcome its new member with all the fanfare and ado possible.

Since this is a very special occasion, go all out and have the birthday invitations printed professionally. Send invitations to newspapers, the mayor, the governor and congressmen, telling one and all of this milestone in life.

The centennial anniversary of life is an opportunity to recall cherished moments and relationships with friends and family. All too seldom in today's society do family and friends scattered about the continent gather together for a birthday celebration. Take this opportunity to make this occasion a tremendous reunion of family and friends from far and wide.

For a party of this size, a very large area will be needed. A room or a tent can be rented to accommodate all the guests. Contact a rental company and you will be surprised at what you can rent. The dishes, tables and tablecloths, silverware, glasses, almost anything for the party can be acquired this way. Paper goods can be used if you do not desire to rent everything.

Decorations for the room need not be elaborate but should be bright and cheerful. Make a cluster of balloons and hang it in the middle of the room. Drape streamers from the center of the room to the corners. A "Happy Birthday" sign can be hung over the table.

Depending on the number of guests, set up enough tables on the side of the room for all the food. Have a separate table for the beverages. Round tables should be set up in the room with a centerpiece on each (fresh or artificial flowers, plants or candles). The tablecloths and napkins on the round tables and buffet table(s) should match.

Food

Shrimp Deviled Eggs

20 eggs	¾ c. chives	3 tbsp. lemon juice
paprika	salt	2 cans shrimp
¾ c. sour cream	pepper	

Cut eggs in half lengthwise and remove yolks. Mash yolks and add sour cream, chives, salt, pepper and lemon juice. Mix well and stuff egg halves. Sprinkle with paprika and top with shrimp.

(makes 40 servings)

Tomato Appetizer Pie

2 9" pie shells, frozen
2½ large tomatoes
  flour
  oil
1 bunch scallions, minced

6 slices Provolone cheese
3 eggs
2 c. grated cheddar cheese
1½ c. heavy cream

Cut tomatoes into ½" thick slices and put aside. Bake the pie shell at 400° F. for 10 minutes. Cool. Combine eggs and cheddar cheese and stir into heavy cream. Dip slices of tomato into flour. Sauté the tomatoes in oil. Sprinkle scallions on the bottom of the pie shells, saving 4 tablespoons. Lay the Provolone cheese over the scallions. Put the tomatoes over the cheese. Pour the cream mixture over the ingredients in the pie shells. Sprinkle the rest of the scallions on top. Bake at 375° F. for about 45 minutes or until the filling is set. Cool a few minutes before cutting.

(Each pie makes 6 to 8 servings)

Marinated Antipasto

cauliflower, cut up into bite-size pieces
broccoli, cut up into bite-size pieces
celery, cut up into bite-size pieces

cherry tomatoes
mushrooms
1 bottle Italian dressing

Marinate the above vegetables overnight in the dressing. Serve in a large bowl.

Turkey

Prepare a large turkey and carve it. Lay the turkey on a platter decorated with parsley and cherry tomatoes. Serve with cranberry sauce and dinner rolls.

For this gala occasion, champagne is in order. Serve it chilled.

Century Cake

3 packages cake mix, any flavor
3 cans ready-made frosting, any flavor

Prepare cake mixes according to package directions, using two 10" fluted pans and one 13" x 9" baking pan. Let cakes cool. Cut down the 13" x 9" cake to 10" x 9". Cut the 10" x 9" cake in half lengthwise to make two cakes 10" x 4½". Using one can of frosting, frost one 10" x 4½" cake completely and lay the other piece on top and frost the entire cake. Melt the other two cans of frosting over low heat one at a time and drizzle over the two fluted cakes. Cover a piece of cardboard 30" x 15" with aluminum foil and lay the three cakes on it to form the number "100" as illustrated.

fig. 1

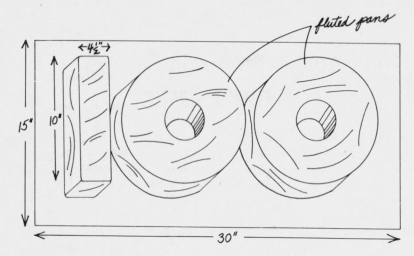

Special Activity

An album with pictures and events for every ten years of the guest of honor's life is a nice memento for this party. A little preparation is involved beforehand to create this album. Start the album with the birth date of the centenarian. Obtain a baby picture and a newspaper headline from the date of birth. Do this for every ten years, including a picture for each decade and a headline from the birthday. To find the newspaper headlines, most libraries keep newspapers on microfilm and the headlines can be researched. Make up the headlines and put them in the album above the picture for the decade. Or, instead of making up the headlines, they can be obtained through mail-order houses advertised in newspapers and magazines. This makes a nice birthday gift and it is certainly well appreciated.

Since this party is a reunion and will bring back many memories, people will do much reminiscing about the good old days. Therefore, this party can combine the special activities from several of the parties mentioned in this book. It might be a good idea to read through the parties from ages 40 and up for some other ideas for this party.

CHAPTER XI

Around the World Through Birthday Parties

How do children in other countries celebrate their birthdays? In many countries it is quite different from the way we celebrate this important event. If you want an unusual birthday party, it can be made following the traditions of a foreign party. All of the information compiled in this chapter was acquired through interviews with people native to the given countries. You may know people of other backgrounds who can tell you of customs in other countries, or you may research other countries' customs in your library.

Brazil

In Brazil, invitations to a birthday party are made by telephone; written invitations are not sent. The parties usually last from four to five hours and the parents of the children are expected to stay.

The people, whether rich or poor, go to extremes for a child's birthday party. They decorate the party room very colorfully and everything is coordinated to go along with a theme. One might have fabric flowers or other types of handmade decorations on the party tables. A small band, clown or magician makes popular entainment for the children.

There are women (usually housewives) who, by word of mouth, are known to specialize in making the different things needed for a birthday party. For instance, one can call a woman and hire her to make hors d'oeuvres, party favors, pastries, candies or the birthday cake, depending on that particular woman's specialty.

There are usually two tables set up for the party. One is for the cake, pastries and other sweets and the other is for the large variety of hors d'oeuvres that are served. The cake is usually a very large layer cake made to feed about 75 people. It has fruits, creams and jellies in it. Sometimes, particularly in the summer, there is fresh fruit on top of it. Two of the more popular pastries served at birthday parties are Bombas (French éclairs) and Napoleons. A sweet that appears at most parties in Brazil is Olho Da Sogra.

Olho Da Sogra
(My Mother-in-Law's Eye)
2 lbs. black dried prunes (pitted)   12 egg yolks
½ lb. sugar   grated coconut (optional)

Make a slit on the side of the prune if it is not already there. Melt sugar and let it cool. When it is cool, mix it with the egg yolks. Put on the heat again and heat until clear. Let cool. If the mixture is not thick enough to use as stuffing for prunes, mix with a little grated coconut to thicken. Put the mixture into the slit in the prune. Place each prune on a miniature cupcake paper.

Israel

In Israel, as in many foreign countries, there are no written invitations. People are invited to a birthday party by word of mouth. All the classmates of the birthday child are usually invited to the party. The relatives are also invited. Therefore the party is generally a large one. It has no time limit.

When the party is for a small child, it is a tradition to have him sit on a chair and to raise him and the chair as many times as he is old plus one for good luck. The chair-raising is usually done by the child's father and uncle or other relative. The birthday child wears a wreath of flowers on his head to mark this special occasion.

The parties are not fancy but there is an abundance of food and drink. Everything is served buffet-style, with a large variety of candies, nuts, raisins and cakes laid out on the table. The children usually sit on the floor to eat and, while they are eating, they play games. Unlike our one Happy Birthday song, the Israelis have several songs they sing in honor of the birthday child.

France

In France, the parties are usually not very elaborate. As a matter of fact, invitations are extended to a few close friends by word of mouth or telephoned instead of written. The party is usually a small one celebrated at 4:00 P.M. which is their daily afternoon snack time. The reason for this is that French people generally eat late and light suppers.

Customarily, there are no special decorations. A fancy cake is used as the birthday cake. Along with the cake, pastries, petits-fours and sandwiches cut in fancy shapes are served.

Petits-Fours

1 package cake mix (any flavor)
1 can ready-made frosting (any flavor)
Prepare cake mix according to package directions, using a jelly roll pan, 15½" x 10½" x 1". Bake at 350° F. for 20 minutes or until toothpick inserted in center comes out dry. Cool. Cut into various shapes with open cookie cutters. Place cake on cake rack with piece of wax paper underneath for excess drippings. Melt ready-made frosting on a low heat and drip on top and sides of cooled cake. Decorate tops with raisins, candy, chips, etc.

The games that are played at French birthday parties are games that the children have in their homes, such as Monopoly® and cards. They even play house or school.

Mexico

A Mexican birthday usually is an all-day party. The house is decorated gaily and colorfully with bright tissue flowers, real flowers and balloons. Music is an important part of the party. Mexican tunes are sometimes played by a mariachi band. There is a very gay and lively atmosphere from the time the birthday child awakes in the morning until bed time.

One of the more common Mexican foods that might be served at a party is tacos. They are very simple to prepare with a taco kit which is available in most supermarkets.

The highlight of a Mexican party is the breaking of the piñata. It was originally made from a clay pot, but can be made from papier maché. For instructions on how to make a piñata, refer to the Let's Play Ball party. Instead of painting the papier maché, glue brightly colored streamers onto it. The piñata is hung from the ceiling of a room or outdoors from a tree. The children take turns trying to break the piñata with a stick while blindfolded. Inside the piñata there is candy which falls to the ground when the piñata is broken.

CHAPTER XII
Through the Year With Birthdays

During any year, there are many holidays and special occasions that can be used as themes for birthday parties. As a matter of fact, every month has either a holiday or special occasion. For each month of the year, we have presented ideas that can be expanded into a party to go along with the significance of a particular birth month.

JANUARY — *Father Time Party*

Food	Round sandwich with numbers of clock written on it, using mustard from squeeze container
Games	Number and time games
Cake	Alarm Clock (round cake with numbers written on with cake decorating gel)
Favor	Toy watches, date books or calendars
Special Activity	
	Make clocks from paper plates; adult party — go back in time and play children's games

FEBRUARY — *Cherry Tree Party*

Food	Peanut butter and cherry preserves sandwich
Games	Historical quiz; relay races with center area as river which people have to cross
Cake	Cherry Cake (two round cakes attached with string licorice stems; leaves are green construction paper)
Favor	Roll up a dollar bill and tie a ribbon around it
Special Activity	
	Trip to historical monument or site

MARCH — *Mardi Gras Party*

Food	Fish sticks and spaghetti
Games	Guessing games
Cake	Masquerade Cake (See Costume Birthday Party)
Favor	Mask
Special Activity	
	Make a costume party and vote on the most original

APRIL — *Backward Birthday Party*

Food	Inside-out sandwiches (piece of bread between two slices of luncheon meat)
Games	Backward spelling bee
Cake	Pineapple Upside-Down Cake
Favor	Pocket or makeup mirror
Special Activity	
	Reverse the schedule of the party (open presents first, etc.), play tricks on guests (*Example:* pinch people's cheeks with lipstick on fingers)

MAY — *The Flowers That Bloom in the Spring Party*

Food	Flower-shaped sandwiches cut with cookie cutters
Games	Games relating to flower names
Cake	Tulip Cake (cut from 13" x 9" pan)
Favor	Small flowerpot with seeds sown in it
Special Activity	
	Plant seeds in flower pot

JUNE — *Hello Sunshine Party*

Food	Open-faced American cheese sandwiches cut into circles and served with orange juice
Games	Relay races and outdoor ball games
Cake	Sunshine Cake (see Outta Sight Birthday Party)
Favor	Book about the sun
Special Activity	
	Have outdoor party (Scavenger or Treasure Hunt)

JULY — *Vacation Party*

Food	Picnic foods (fried chicken, potato salad, cole slaw)
Games	Any ball games
Cake	Beach Ball Cake (see Let's Play Ball Party)
Favor	Pail and shovel
Special Activity	
	Take guests on "vacation" to the beach for a picnic

AUGUST — *Splash Party*

Food	Hot dogs and hamburgers
Games	Water games
Cake	Swimming Pool Cake (round cake frosted brown on sides, blue on top with tongue depressor for a diving board)
Favor	Beach balls
Special Activity	
	Have party at pool or beach

SEPTEMBER — *Three R's Party*

Food	Alphabet soup
Games	Pencil and paper games, spelling or math bees
Cake	Addition Cake (13" x 9" cake; write $1 + 1 = 2$)
Favor	Pencil case or pad and pencil
Special Activity	
	Give "lesson" on making a craft

OCTOBER — *Discover America Party*

Food	Cream cheese and jelly sandwich [spread half of sandwich with red jelly (raspberry) and half with blue (blueberry)]
Games	Games relating to the states
Cake	Flag Cake (13" x 9" cake designed like American Flag)
Favor	Small flags
Special Activity	
	Make American Flag placemat (see Superheroes Party)

NOVEMBER — *Mayflower Party*

Food	Turkey sandwiches
Games	Create as many words as possible from "Mayflower" or "Thanksgiving"
Cake	Boat Cake (cut a 13" x 9" cake to look like a boat)
Favor	Plymouth Rock paperweight
Special Activity	
	Make Plymouth Rock favor by decorating small rocks

DECEMBER — *Winter Wonderland Party*

Food	Soup and sandwich
Games	Snowball fight (indoors) with cotton balls
Cake	Mitten Cake (use hand as pattern to cut cake)
Favor	Mitt Washcloth (see Let's Play Ball Party)
Special Activity	
	Take guests ice skating

CHAPTER XIII

Around the World in 52 Weeks

For every week in the year, there is a holiday or special event somewhere in the world. These can be used as themes for birthday parties. Included are special occasions and a theme idea for each week of the year.

WEEK	EVENT	PARTY THEME
JANUARY		
1	The Mummers' Day Parade (Philadelphia)	Musical Instrument
2	The First Balloon Ascension (Philadelphia)	Balloon
3	Anniversary of first basketball game (Springfield, Massachusetts)	Sports
4	Australia Independence Day	Marching Band (see Strike Up the Band)
FEBRUARY		
1	Anniversary of first Winter Olympic games	Indoor Olympics (see Way Out Games)
2	Battleship Day (Maine)	Ship Ahoy!
3	Gambia Independence Day (Africa)	Blue, Green and Red
4	Longfellow's Birthday	Poetry
MARCH		
1	Alamo Day (Texas)	Frontier
2	The Blizzard of 1888	Snow (see Winter Wonderland Party)
3	Bird Day (Iowa)	A bird or birds
4	Greek Independence Day	Greek Festival
APRIL		
1	Anniversary of the establishment of the United States Mint	Money
2	Humane Day; anniversary of the incorporation of American Society for the Prevention of Cruelty to Animals	Your Favorite Pet
3	Queen Margrethe's birthday, observed in Denmark	Queens and Kings

WEEK	EVENT	PARTY THEME
4	Secretaries' Day honoring women in the secretarial field	What do I want to be when I grow up?
MAY		
1	Lei Day — a Hawaiian flower festival	Flower (see The Flowers That Bloom in the Spring)
2	Anniversary of the presentation of the idea of Book Week	Book Review
3	Lindbergh Flight Day — the first successful non-stop solo transatlantic flight	Transportation
4	Joan of Arc Day — she brought victory to France and ended the Hundred Years' War with England	Soldier
JUNE		
1	Children's Festival Day observed in the People's Republic of China	Street Carnival
2	Flag Day	Red, White and Blue
3	Organization of the World Court	Here Comes the Judge
4	Grand Prix of Belgium	Auto Race
JULY		
1	American Stamp Day — anniversary of the issuance of the first United States postage stamps	Let's Play Post Office
2	Bastille Day — French national hoilday	Crepes
3	The National Cherry Festival (Michigan)	Cherry (see Cherry Tree Party)
4	Peruvian Independence Day	Foods from Around the World
AUGUST		
1	Premiere of Talking Pictures	Movies of the Past (see Movies at Home Party)
2	Indian Day (Massachusetts)	Cowboys and Indians (see Wild West Party)
3	Hawaii Statehood Day	Luau (see Hawaiian Feast)

WEEK	EVENT	PARTY THEME
4	Liberian Flag Day (Liberia)	Flags from Around the World
SEPTEMBER		
1	Midwest Old Settlers and Threshers Reunion (Iowa)	Old-Fashioned Party
2	Anniversary of the opening of the first school of journalism at the University of Missouri	Let's Play School (see Three R's Party)
3	Mexican Declaration of Independence Day (comparable to July 4 in the United States)	Mexican Fiesta
4	Good Neighbor Day (United States)	Block Party
OCTOBER		
1	National Sports Day (Lesotho, formerly Basutoland)	Games
2	Fire Prevention Day — anniversary of the Chicago Fire (United States)	Fire! Fire! False Alarm!
3	Apple Tuesday (St. Louis)	Fruit
4	National Magic Day — honoring magicians	Magic
NOVEMBER		
1	Author's Day honoring writers of American literature	Famous Authors
2	Tree Festival Day (Tunisia)	Tree Planting
3	Equal Opportunity Day — anniversary of Lincoln's Gettysburg Address (National Cemetery)	Debate
4	John F. Kennedy Day (Massachusetts)	American President
DECEMBER		
1	Pan American Health Day (United States)	Health Food
2	Beach Day or Blessing of the Waters Day (Family Day); the beginning of beach season (Uruguay)	Indoor Water Party (see Splash Party)
3	Boston Tea Party Day	Tea Party
4	Birthday of frontiersman and guide Kit Carson	Pioneer (see Wild West Party)

Suggested Gifts

Ages 1-5

Books
Bulletin board
Cars and trucks
Chalkboard and chalk
Crayons and coloring books
Crystal Climbers®
Doctor kit
Doll
Doll carriage or stroller
Dominoes
Educational games
Etch A Sketch®
Juvenile bed sheet and pillow case
Juvenile dinnerware set
Juvenile table and chairs
Large beads to string
Lego blocks®
Letter or number flash cards
Magnetic alphabet letters and
  numbers with magnetic board
Matching games
Monogrammed article of clothing
Picture lotto game
Plastic animals or people

Play cobbler apron
Play-Dough®
Pull toy
Puppet
Purse
Push button or battery
  operated toy
Puzzles
Records
Riding toy with or without pedals
Set of watercolor felt-tip pens
Set of watercolor paints
Stacking toy
Stuffed animal
Swimming equipment
Tinker Toy construction toys
Toy clock
Toy instrument
Toy pots and pans
Toy stove, sink or refrigerator
Toy tea set
Wagon
Water toys
Wooden blocks

Ages 6-15

Activity books
Arts and crafts toys
Beach towel
Bicycle accessories
Books
Building toys
Camera
Cars and trucks
Children's pocket calculator
Clay
Crazy knee socks
Decal T-shirt
Educational game
Electric trains or accessories
Fashion dolls and accessories
Globe
Hats, scarves, mittens or gloves
Jewelry
Jewelry box

Kite
Lunch box
Money
Monogrammed article of clothing
Personalized switch plate
Portable electronic game
Poster
Puzzles
Records
School bag
Shoe bag
Sports equipment
Tape recorder
Transistor radio
Umbrella
Wall-hanging toothbrush holder
Watch

Ages 16-19

Baby bracelet
Bangle bracelet
Bicycle accessories
Books
Cologne, dusting powder,
    scented soaps
Decal T-shirt
Electric beauty aid
Electric shaver
Gold chain
Hobby accessories
Jewelry box

Monogrammed article of clothing
Monogrammed stationery
Pen and pencil set
Pendant watch
Pocket calculator
Portable electronic game
Poster
Record or tape case
Records or tapes
Scarf
Sports equipment
Typewriter
Zodiac pendant or keychain

Ages 20 and up

Belt buckle
Binoculars
Books
Business card paperweight
Change purse
Coin collecting accessories
Cologne
Cookbooks and cooking accessories
Desk accessories
Dinner for two
Electric train set
Flowers or plant
Framed picture or print
Games
Gift certificate to a beauty salon
Hobby accessories
Jewelry
Keychain with or without flashlight
Large print book or newspaper
Lightweight luggage
Lucite® items
Magazine or newspaper
    subscription
Magnifying glass
Money clip
Monogrammed article of clothing
Monogrammed stationery
Necktie
Needlework kit
Passport case
Personalized auto mat

Personalized checkbook cover
Personalized coffee mugs
Personalized license plate frame
Picture frame or album
Pillbox
Pipe
Pipe rack
Plastic playing cards
Pocket address or date book
Pocket calculator
Pocket watch
Printer's tray and small items
    to put in it
Purse mirror
Records or tapes
Risqué gifts
Sewing book and accessories
Sports equipment
Stamp collecting accessories
Theater tickets
Tie tac
Tools
Travel accessories
Travel alarm clock
Travel iron
Wall calendar
Wall clock with large numerals
Waterproof scarf or hat
Wine rack

9593